It's Not You,
It's Me

It's Not You, It's Me

THE POETRY OF BREAKUP

Edited and with an introduction by
JERRY WILLIAMS

THE OVERLOOK PRESS
NEW YORK

for Jenni Ferrari-Adler and Juliet Grames

This edition first published in hardcover in the United States in 2010 by
The Overlook Press, Peter Mayer Publishers, Inc.
141 Wooster Street
New York, NY 10012

Cataloging-in-Publication Data is available from the Library of Congress

Book design and type formatting by Bernard Schleifer
Manufactured in the United States of America
FIRST EDITION
2 4 6 8 10 9 7 5 3 1
ISBN 978-1-59020-282-1

Contents

II. In the Middle of the Storm

III. The Aftermath

Introduction

POETRY IS MY FAVORITE FORM OF HUMAN EXPRESSION ON EARTH. BREAKUPS ARE my least favorite. So why am I introducing a book that intermingles both splendor and ruin? Let me try to explain.

I have endured four major breakups in my life. Each one nearly killed me. Without a two-month grief regimen of inspiring poetry, unintentional dieting, weightlifting, sofa catatonia, and the potentially detrimental miracle of anti-depressant and anti-anxiety medication, I might never have survived. What's more, a number of lesser disintegrations have compromised my brittle nervous system. By now, I've spent so much time in the throes of dissolution that I must certainly have achieved a keener understanding of the process, if not an advanced degree of expertise.

When I see a breakup on the horizon, I grease myself down for the inevitable descent into hell. I quickly arrange for a therapist and pills. I warn my friends. I stock up on bananas and peanut butter, and I place the elegant volumes of, say, Mark Strand and the poet Ai on the nightstand. I post the gym hours on the refrigerator. When I'm inside a breakup the business of life slows to a crawl, and the thought of one person occupies my entire imagination. I doubt the ragged wisdom I've accrued is worth the mental and physical toll exacted by the experience. It's like saying you're really good at getting struck by lightning.

Biographically speaking, Debra came first. We met in high school in Dayton, Ohio. We treated each other sweetly for a long time, but she grew to resent my weirdo literary aspirations, and the relationship turned gory. She started cheating on me with two different guys, and instead of getting rid of me she kept me around as a witness to her infinite need to feel wanted. I can remember lying on the floor with my ear to the telephone, consumed by jealousy and shaking like a condemned prisoner, as she recounted the prurient details of her betrayal. At the time, my parents were howling through a divorce. My father had gone bankrupt, and my mother and I moved into a one-bedroom apartment with my two older sisters and my three-year-old niece. My father ended up living in his car.

Around Christmas, the distaff side of my family kicked me out of the apartment, and I moved in with a friend. The depression that resulted from converging misfortunes brought me to my knees. I couldn't get out of bed. I couldn't eat. I couldn't breathe. I felt as though I'd developed a psychic tumor. I wanted to throw myself under a bus in order to annihilate the vessel that offered shelter to such unrelenting pain. Luckily, I'd been in trouble with the police (thievery, vandalism), and my court-appointed therapist put me on an anti-depressant that gave me cottonmouth and made my lower back hurt. The drug saved me from complete collapse, and I avoided the state mental ward, but the way I would now live in the world changed forever. Anguish had taken up residence in a dim, airless room just down the hall, and the door could fly open at any moment and suck my fragile life inside.

Debra haunted the fringes for a few more years—better the devil you know, I suppose—then she pirated off into her own separate future. I read a fair amount of poetry during this period, the only communication that could touch my panic and melancholy. I virtually inhabited Stephen Berg's poem "Listener," in which a man and woman end their relationship over the phone. The narrator's frantic reaction to the facts rings true. His unraveling culminates in the contemplation of advancing shock troops and birdsong. Amy Gerstler's "Fuck You Poem #45" reflected my rage. The precision of her language slashes her rival to ribbons. And Denis Johnson's poem "After Mayakovsky" nearly gave me the strength "to address / the ages and history and the universe" and say to Debra, "I swear you'll never see my face again."

At the University of Dayton, I met Amanda, a political science major. We dated for a total of five years—nine months of which we lived together in Los Angeles. Much of the relationship was a disaster. I lied and cheated and punched walls, and I drank like a billy goat eats. We broke up three times, once in a parking lot in Las Vegas, once or twice through the mail during an interval of geographic separation. I kept telling myself that something was waiting for me around the bend or over the next ridge and when I found it I needed to be alone. Somehow, I followed Amanda to New Jersey when she got accepted to graduate school at Princeton.

Soon after we arrived, I found myself browsing the faintly-lit stacks at the university library and came across Robert Kelly's book *Under Words*. The poem "I want to tell you why husbands stop loving wives" jumped off the page, grabbed me by the throat, and forced me to confess that Amanda and I needed to "die to each other and live." I provoked the final disconnection as we sat in her car one evening, right around the corner from the library where I had recently taken a job searching for lost books. Three weeks later I tried to retract the pronouncement, but she was already seeing someone else. I cried and pleaded and confessed all my sins in a convulsion of jealousy—to no avail. Clearly, I got what I deserved: two years of isolation and celibacy. In his poem "The Pure Loneliness," Michael Ryan describes, in his own blood, the nemesis I would face: "Late at night when you're so lonely, / your shoulders curl toward the center of your body, / you call no one and you don't call out. // This is dignity. This is the pure loneliness / that made Christ think he was God."

When Amanda cut off all contact, I dug a hide against depression's nuclear winter. I located a therapist and a pharmacologist, and I bought myself a good pillow. I started going to the gym in order to burn off the agitation that my agony produced, lifting weights and riding the exercise bike like a grim-faced, self-flagellating Travis Bickle in Scorcese's *Taxi Driver*. At work, I would sometimes speed-walk down to the lockable restroom on B floor of the library, drop to the dirty tile, and rip through forty or fifty push-ups with my eyes tightly closed. The tasks I performed in my job required autonomy and quiet, thus my co-workers barely noticed that my speaking voice had dwindled to a stage whisper. Sadness filled every crevice of every moment. At home, my body ached and my mind continually drowned in its own poison. The past and the future seemed to disappear in a haze of dread. I couldn't remember a time when I felt right and I couldn't envision a time when I would ever feel right again.

My therapist reasoned that breakups tapped into the privation of my childhood and triggered the mania, but awareness of this diagnosis only made the pain worse—because after a breakup or divorce knowledge is powerlessness. Rationality starves. At such times, poetry might be the only music we can hear. Each poem leads us out beyond our afflictions and sends us back to ourselves less saturated with fear.

In his lyric "Heavy Trash," Mark Halliday suggests that "some endings never end." The memento set ablaze in the kitchen sink goes on burning forever. On the other hand, the body will often allow the mind to heal, time being the only effective cure for a depressive illness. Consequently, I recovered. I made a list and mounted a belated effort to transform my life. I'd flunked out of the University of Dayton and if I didn't want to labor at menial jobs for the next forty years, I had to return to school. Fortunately, Vermont College offered a low-residency undergraduate degree, so I boarded a train at Penn Station in the middle of January, bound for Montpelier and a vital second chance.

Within two years, the college presented me with a diploma and a girlfriend, my dear Annie, the most beautiful person I had ever met.

After six brooding months of long-distance courtship, we decided to move in together. We took up residence in my perilously tiny apartment in a converted Victorian house in Princeton. She found work as a nanny, and I continued slaving away at the library. Crushing immaturity and an inability to communicate endangered the relationship almost immediately. Nevertheless, we lived together for nine months. The apartment walls started closing in, and no amount of occupying the space in shifts could alleviate the tension. Mistakes were made, as the politician says. When the University of Arizona admitted me to the M.F.A. program, I sent Annie back to her hometown of Lowell, Massachusetts. I couldn't bear dragging her westward for the sake of an ailing union. Ultimately, though, I regretted having made this choice, and I spent the next decade trying to recant and reclaim the first real love of my life—again, to no avail.

Getting ready for relocation to Arizona meant packing my belongings in the back of a used Ford Ranger and bungee-cording the mass of objects beneath a sea-green tarp. Pretending to adulthood, I included as many of my possessions as possible. Then, emotionally and physically worn out from all the lifting and dragging, I returned to the apartment one last time to take a quick shower and make sure I hadn't overlooked anything. In the corner of the bathroom, a pair of Annie's empty little running shoes set off a spasm of nostalgia, and I promptly lunged for the toilet and threw up. At that moment, I came to the realization that I would never survive the trip alone, so I invited my friend Jonathan Ames to join me and help keep me sane. Thankfully, he agreed. After the expedition, he planned to fly back to the east coast and finish work on his second novel.

I collected Jonathan at his parents' house in northern New Jersey, where he'd been staying for the past few months. Once he stowed his backpack in the space I created under the tarp, we headed straight for Interstate 87; merged onto I-78; traversed the Pennsylvania Turnpike; and then picked up I-70, which would take us all the way to my long-lost mother's government-subsidized apartment in Dayton, Ohio. We spent the night there and woke the next morning to heaping plates of homemade gravy and biscuits, a wonderful southern delicacy that reminded me of the anomalous pleasant expression of my childhood. After breakfast, Jonathan and I climbed into my royal blue truck and followed the recently constructed interchange to I-70. I started feeling agitated around Terre Haute, Indiana; despondent in Decatur, Illinois; and completely wretched when the truck ran aground on the outskirts of St. Louis during a violent rainstorm. We disembarked at the first motel we could find.

That night, as my friend slept soundly in his bed, I lay awake and thin-skinned in mine. The closing lines of Kim Addonizio's poem "Ex-Boyfriends" captured the expansiveness of my desolation. With burning eyes, I watched the grimy walls absorb "the faint restless arcs / of headlights from the freeway's passing trucks, // the big rigs that travel and travel, / hauling their loads between cities, warehouses, / following the familiar routes of their loneliness." The loss of a loved one hurts differently when you're on the road. The scenery moves by so fast you can barely tell one shape from another. When you finally drop anchor and look at the living world up close, everything seems as bereft as you are.

Jonathan had hoped to do some sightseeing during our crossing, so I made an effort to act the part of the adventurous companion, but an inner tremor and slack facial muscles gave me away. Despite the medication I dutifully consumed, a frenzied despair took hold of my tender physiognomy. I was sucking all the air out of the cab of the truck without even breathing. Poor Jonathan did his best to distract me, but misery mixed with transience turns out a mean cocktail. Regardless, we paused at some sort of Elvis Presley Museum in Missouri and later waded through an ocean of tall green grass in Kansas. At every possible stop, I rooted out the nearest payphone and called Annie collect. In the single greatest act of selfless compassion I have ever witnessed, she would stay on the phone for as long as I needed, devoid of spite or uncertainty, even though I had pulled up stakes without "the proper handling / of goodbye," to borrow a phrase from Linda Gregg's poem "The Night Before Leaving." The pain of that memory is so perfectly and beautifully intact I cannot fight off a crying jag as I watch these words appear on my computer screen. No joke—Annie belongs in the Breakup Hall of Fame: the woman who offered comfort to a man who almost destroyed her happiness.

Interstate 70 led us to Boulder, Colorado, where we spent the night at a mutual friend's house. In the morning, we crusaded west into Utah. Jonathan seemed so excited to see the unearthly terrain of the Beehive State, which I had described to him during a rare patch of clarity, having myself experienced the grandeur of the many canyons and salt flats on a previous cross-country drive. As we approached the Utah state line, my ass started to itch. I tried to ignore the irritation, but the itching evolved into stinging and the stinging into torment. I asked Jonathan to pull into a gas station around Fruita,

Colorado, and I ran to the restroom, locked the door, climbed up on the sink, and inspected my posterior in the mirror. Both cheeks were inflamed and erupting. In my fog of sorrow, I assumed the worst: gangrene, leprosy, that flesh-eating disease everyone was talking about.

I toddled back to the truck in the blazing sun and informed Jonathan that I might need to go to the hospital. He suggested I call Annie, so I seized the payphone near the ice dispenser and jabbed in the numbers. She said, "Honey, it's only a heat rash. Don't be upset. Go to the closest pharmacy and buy some Desitin. Now, that's for diaper rash, but you've got the same thing, essentially. And if you have a pair of loose-fitting shorts, put those on, and change your underwear." Jonathan located a K-Mart in Fruita, and I grimaced through the main entrance and bought extra large sweat pants, boxer shorts, and a tube of Desitin. I retired to a bathroom stall in the rear of the store and applied cream to rump. Then I put on the boxers and sweats and tossed my old underwear in the trash. Standing next to the pickup in the parking lot, Jonathan maintained an appropriately solemn countenance. "I've finally hit bottom," I said, "full-blown infantilization," which made it okay to laugh because neither of us could have invented a more fitting comeuppance for our fleeing narrator.

Surprisingly, we did wind up visiting the high desert of Arches National Park. We listened to the overwhelming silence of Natural Bridges National Monument. We gaped at the enormous, isolated sandstone rocks rising above the Valley of the Gods. We purchased handmade jewelry on the Navajo Nation Indian Reservation in Arizona. Although I remember feeling unable to experience this magnificence with anything approaching gusto, perhaps I'm a better man for not having bailed out altogether. Jonathan drove most of the way down the span of Interstate 10, and when we spotted Tucson in the distance the sensation of coming to the end of the world, the end of America anyway, threw my stomach on its side. I let myself surrender.

Jonathan lent a hand in unloading the truck in front of yet another tiny dwelling, and later I dropped him off at the airport, probably shook his hand, and that was it. Then, as in Steve Orlen's poem "A Man Alone," I tried "to summon up / Who I was before the bed was full with woman." Two months of the gym, the sauna, the swimming pool, and the sun, and I felt almost human. Reading the verse of my future professors—Richard Shelton, Jane Miller, Alison Hawthorne Deming, and Steve Orlen—suggested a sense of approaching community. Annie helped by calling every few nights and acting like she was still my girlfriend. I can even summon up a sort of fondness for those months now, a fondness for survival.

After graduating from the University of Arizona, I couldn't get a real teaching position (not enough publication), and I couldn't imagine looking for a straight job. In the past, I had worked as a landscaper, typist, bartender, delivery driver of automobile parts, cashier, telephone solicitor, and dishwasher. The idea of walking back into anything resembling that way of life frightened the hell out of me. Thus, I applied to the only creative writing doctoral program whose deadline for admissions hadn't passed—Oklahoma State University. All my friends said I was crazy, and the woman I'd been seeing, a divorced undergraduate chemistry major named Melissa, expressed shock that I would consider leaving town for something so shallow as my career. Anyhow, I got accepted, and I decided to go. I flipped through the same road atlas that brought me to Arizona and located Stillwater, Oklahoma, on the map. I thought, How bad can it be? I'll tell you how bad it can be: I feel like I got a tattoo of a dead horse on my back that took four years to complete.

A semester locked inside the poky of the Bible Belt, pining away for my girlfriend, and I agreed to let her transfer to Oklahoma State and move into the cheap two-bedroom house I'd rented near campus. I flew to Tucson and helped pack her Ford Tracer, and we took I-40, across New Mexico and Texas, directly to Stillwater. She started crying outside Albuquerque and pretty much didn't stop for five months. She missed her friends, and she couldn't believe she'd uprooted herself for a guy she wasn't even married to. If someone follows you to a whole other state, the pressure brought to bear can destroy the relationship. She might blame you for anything from a long line at the post office to sour milk, and you will devotedly soak up that blame like a desert convicted of selling water to sharks—until you explode. Jack Gilbert's poem "Walking Home Across the Island" mirrored our predicament's bare-knuckled distress: "Again we have come / to a place where I rail and she suffers and the moon / does not rise. We have only each other, / but I am shouting inside the rain / and she is crying like a wounded animal, / knowing there is no place to turn. It is hard / to understand how we could be brought here by love." Sadly, I never got the chance to show these words to Melissa, words that might have halted our demise. She had already cried her eyes out.

In the month of May, Melissa and I decided that we should spend some time apart, so she retreated to Arizona for the summer. In reality, time apart turned into a half-assed breakup because she commenced dating her neighbor, a fellow chemistry major, who had stopped by to put salve on her emotional injuries. Don't be surprised if one day this guy wins the Nobel Prize for discovering a formula for consoling the inconsolable. Bitter humor aside, this new development opened the door to that dim, airless room of anguish just down the hall. I was in serious trouble. My dignity dissolved in a puff of lost hope, and I made a few beseeching phone calls to Melissa that I regret. I felt continuously aware of my declining mental state, and I am ashamed to admit that allusions to self-murder crept into the pages of my journal. Such ideation had nothing to do with Melissa *per se*, though I certainly remained obsessed. I had simply reached a point where I could no longer tolerate the suffering that my rusted-out romantic attachments provoked, nor the grueling, isolated gaps in between.

According to the many textbooks, depressive episodes get worse and worse over the course of one's lifetime. Then again, my grief regimen had reached a level of grotesque perfection that would have impressed Emily Post. I borrowed a friend's doctor and acquired the necessary pills. I subscribed to HBO, indented the sofa, and gazed at the television for hours on end, making sure to change the channel at the first sign of sex or sentimentality. I was starving, but the notion of food seemed revolting. Every morning, I drank a cup of coffee with my meds, drove up to the reservoir, and jogged its three-mile circumference. I went home and read Sharon Olds and Tony Hoagland with the TV on mute. In the afternoon, I hit the gym to lift weights. I suppose I actually wanted to harm myself, to bring the interior menace to the anxious surface.

Whether or not Melissa and I were compatible long-term, I refused to forgive myself for not utterly enjoying her company during our time together. Donna Masini's poem "Longing" righteously portrays this way of thinking and then reveals the inevitable consequences: "But just / now I thought of him, I thought yes, the arm. / His arm. His *arm*. / Now that it's over it is luminous again." Comparable torturous contemplation brought me to the dank and stifling weight room day after day to receive the sacrament of oblivion.

By the end of the summer, my symptoms faded and my ability to focus returned. Over the next three years, I finished my course work at Oklahoma State, forked over my poetry dissertation, and fled with my degree in hand. After two years as a Visiting Professor at a small liberal arts college in Rhode Island, I finally published a book and landed a tenure-track job at a small liberal arts college in Manhattan—Mecca to the lonesome scribbler. While sitting in an aromatic coffee bar on Lexington Avenue one Saturday afternoon, I came up with the idea for this anthology. A seasoned proponent of turning ordeal into art, I marched back to my tiny studio on 65th Street and began paging through the dozens of poetry collections that dominated my shelves. I found half the poems you're about to read in my very own living quarters. Subconsciously, I must have been preparing this anthology ever since I was sixteen years old and swiped my first book from the library. I've always been drawn to breakup and divorce poems. They have quite suddenly materialized in the middle of my life—always at the right time—like a forgotten five-dollar bill in your jacket pocket. I kept a mental catalogue.

When I decided to attempt this compilation of rescue poems, I established a few ground rules: (1) the poets still had to be alive; (2) they had to be female and/or male, gay and/or straight, minority and/or majority; and (3) the work needed to be non-therapeutic yet transformative, hard-hitting, enlightening, emotionally varied, wide-ranging technically, and either clear-cut or discursive. In the end, however, I simply went for the poems that "[make] the stomach believe," to quote Tim O'Brien's *The Things They Carried*.

After I finished off the books in my apartment, I took the subway to Poets House (when it was still located on Spring Street) and plowed through the collections of over a hundred poets whose work I loved or thought I might love. I quickly came to the realization that either you write breakup or divorce poems or you don't; either you strip mine that land or you leave it to the trees. Perhaps art mirrors life in this instance. After a breakup or divorce, some people just pick up and move on—with dignity and healthful ease and a slightly mournful smile. Others return, over and over, to the cordoned-off nostalgic scene, like victims of a life-altering crime, asking the wind and dust for understanding.

I have arranged the poems in three sections for easy reference and self-identification: One Foot Out the Door, In the Middle of the Storm, and The Aftermath. I dearly hope you haven't fallen victim to breakup or divorce, but if you have, or someone you know is suffering, I have done my best to make these pages sing and scream and darken and flash. Here, you will not find false hope, but the real hope of colliding with genuineness. You will find wisdom, redemption, anger, and plenty of gallows humor (so feel free to laugh out loud). Whether the unfortunate life experience of breakup or divorce dwells in your past, present, or future, the beauty of the language will take your mind off your mind and bathe your body in recuperative light. I have done my best to gather the poems that will always treat you right.

Modern Love: I

By this he knew she wept with waking eyes:
That, at his hand's light quiver by her head,
The strange low sobs that shook their common bed
Were called into her with a sharp surprise,
And strangled mute, like little gaping snakes,
Dreadfully venomous to him. She lay
Stone-still, and the long darkness flowed away
With muffled pulses. Then, as midnight makes
Her giant heart of Memory and Tears
Drink the pale drug of silence, and so beat
Sleep's heavy measure, they from head to feet
Were moveless, looking through their dead black years,
By vain regret scrawled over the blank wall.
Upon their marriage-tomb, the sword between;
Each wishing for the sword that severs all.

—GEORGE MEREDITH, 1862

I

One Foot Out the Door

PRIVILEGE OF BEING
ROBERT HASS

Many are making love. Up above, the angels
in the unshaken ether and crystal of human longing
are braiding one another's hair, which is strawberry blond
and the texture of cold rivers. They glance
down from time to time at the awkward ecstasy—
it must look to them like featherless birds
splashing in the spring puddle of a bed—
and then one woman, she is about to come,
peels back the man's shut eyelids and says,
look at me, and he does. Or is it the man
tugging the curtain rope in that dark theater?
Anyway, they do, they look at each other;
two beings with evolved eyes, rapacious,
startled, connected at the belly in an unbelievably sweet
lubricious glue, stare at each other,
and the angels are desolate. They hate it. They shudder pathetically
like lithographs of Victorian beggars
with perfect features and alabaster skin hawking rags
in the lewd alleys of the novel.
All of creation is offended by this distress.
It is like the keening sound the moon makes sometimes,
rising. The lovers especially cannot bear it,
it fills them with unspeakable sadness, so that
they close their eyes again and hold each other, each
feeling the mortal singularity of the body
they have enchanted out of death for an hour or so,
and one day, running at sunset, the woman says to the man,
I woke up feeling so sad this morning because I realized
that you could not, as much as I love you,
dear heart, cure my loneliness,
wherewith she touched his cheek to reassure him

that she did not mean to hurt him with this truth.
And the man is not hurt exactly,
he understands that life has limits, that people
die young, fail at love,
fail of their ambitions. He runs beside her, he thinks
of the sadness they have gasped and crooned their way out of
coming, clutching each other with old, invented
forms of grace and clumsy gratitude, ready
to be alone again, or dissatisfied, or merely
companionable like the couples on the summer beach
reading magazine articles about intimacy between the sexes
to themselves, and to each other,
and to the immense, illiterate, consoling angels.

SWEET RUIN
TONY HOAGLAND

Maybe that is what he was after,
my father, when he arranged, ten years ago,
to be discovered in a mobile home
with a woman named Roxanne, an attractive,
recently divorced masseuse.

He sat there, he said later, in the middle
of a red, imitation-leather sofa,
with his shoes off and a whiskey in his hand,
filling up with a joyful kind of dread—
like a swamp, filling up with night,

—while my mother hammered on the trailer door
with a muddy, pried-up stone,
then smashed the headlights of his car,
drove home,
and locked herself inside.

He paid the piper, was how he put it,
because he wanted to live,
and at the time knew no other way
than to behave like some blind and willful beast,
—to make a huge mistake, like a big leap

into space, as if following
a music that required dissonance
and a plunge into the dark.
That is what he tried to tell me,
the afternoon we talked,

as he reclined in his black chair,
divorced from the people in his story
by ten years and a heavy cloud of smoke.
Trying to explain how a man could come
to a place where he has nothing else to gain
unless he loses everything. So he
louses up his work, his love, his own heart.
He hails disaster like a cab. And years later,
when the storm has descended
and rubbed his face in the mud of himself,

he stands again and looks around,
strangely thankful just to be alive,
oddly jubilant—as if he had been granted
the answer to his riddle,
or as if the question

had been taken back. Perhaps
a wind is freshening the grass,
and he can see now, as for the first time,
the softness of the air between the blades. The pleasure
built into a single bending leaf.

Maybe then he calls it, in a low voice
and only to himself, *Sweet Ruin*.
And maybe only because I am his son,
I can hear just what he means. How
even at this moment, even when the world

seems so perfectly arranged, I feel
a force prepared to take it back.
Like a smudge on the horizon. Like a black spot
on the heart. How one day soon,
I might take this nervous paradise,

bone and muscle of this extraordinary life,
and with one deliberate gesture,
like a man stepping on a stick,
break it into halves. But less gracefully

than that. I think there must be something wrong
with me, or wrong with strength, that I would
break my happiness apart
simply for the pleasure of the sound.
The sound the pieces make. What is wrong

with peace? I couldn't say.
But, sweet ruin, I can hear you.
There is always the desire.
Always the cloud, suddenly present
and willing to oblige.

TELL ME, BLACK HEART

Maxine Kumin

Tell me, black heart, twelve white lies.
Let separate cars be our disguise.
Unpack the thin bags of the exiled
each time in the out-of-season inn
where love feeds us like insulin
and summer chintz is glazed and mild.
Stuff my head with alibis.
Tell me, black heart, twelve white lies.

Take two bodies, Davy Jones.
Drink them down to lazybones.
Take bourbon in a toothbrush glass
while the ocean tongues the shore
ten thousand times tonight before
a squall drives off the striper bass
and washes up new lucky stones.
Take two bodies, Davy Jones.

Small comfort that we are not drowned.
Beached and flapping, run aground,
we wake as fresh as children do.
Morning's misty, noon's a ghost.
Rain falls farther up the coast.
Checkout time is half-past two.
Lovers lie here safe and sound.
Small comfort that we are not drowned.

Tell me, black heart, twelve white lies.
Stuff my head with alibis.
Let the gusting east wind chip
splinters from the opposing roof.

Let the seagulls cry reproof.
Our bed rocks like a mooring slip.
Doubt raps twice behind my eyes.
Tell me, black heart, twelve white lies.

I WANT TO TELL YOU WHY HUSBANDS STOP LOVING WIVES

ROBERT KELLY

I want to tell you why husbands stop loving wives
there is a tearing
always a tearing of our hearts
into the geography of Projection
and what is most close to us must
always be found out there
                              and when the wife
is a valve of the husband's heart
and he can't really tell
her cunt from the pie on the table and the sweet
filmy curtains dancing in her windows
and all is one lovely lovely landscape
of intimate dailiness then
Christ stands up in his heart and says Get out
of her, *lech lecha*,
what is most intimate
is already you and you
must find her outside again
for a man must leave wife and father and children
to follow the Me that is himself
through the fervid gethsemanis of adultery
up the bleak hill of divorce.
And night after night the husband
hears that in his head or his heart.
Let this cup pass, and let me drink
always from the warm brown coffee mug she gave me,
let my hours count themselves her servant
and let her stand at the door at nightfall
reclaiming me back from the abstract day.
Let me love this woman

for I love her as I love my life.
And the harsh Christ of the heart says That
is why you must leave her. For every
man who studies to save his life
will lose it. And he
is implacable. The husband
in secret agonies of fantasy
sees her betraying him, sees himself
betraying her with all of her friends,
waitresses, stewardesses, actresses,
anyone at all. He speaks shyly
or she speaks shyly
of other loves and open marriages
and all the bandaids that fall away
night after night and the wound
speaks in him again. He hurls himself on her
desperate to ignite his own passion
to love her once more as he did when she was other.
But his head is turned wrong way round.
He loves where they have been and where they are.
He does not love her future.
Long ago he stopped knowing his way into her dreams
her secrets her subtle rhythms of self-disclosure.
They have feasts. They have friends.
They talk about children.
She knows it all. She has always known it
and pieces her day together from the merest signs.
For Christ talks in her too,
a Christ who wants her for her own:
woman, you belong to no one;
I gave you sun to be continuous
and night and rain
and you need no more.
They all have voices, they all
have arms. To belong
to him is to belong to society,

to Caesar—is that what you want?
And sometimes it is what she wants:
that it all could be done once for all
and life a gentle long echoing
of her first shy assent. But the voice
that hounds her says
Look at him—he brings
hardly the half of him to your bed.
He loves you too well, and you
have become landscape: Even your storms
are common in his well known sky,
like a thunderhead heavy, handsome
over the brow of his own familiar hill.
You belong to your contract
as he does. Nothing
but what *I* do is done only once.
Everything else is again.
Die to each other and live.

CURSE FOUR: ORDERS FOR THE END OF TIME
CYNTHIA HUNTINGTON

> "Whoever is alone will stay alone a long time."
> —RILKE, "Autumn Day"

Time will stop here. A man with a suitcase
going out and coming in. Opening a car door.
Whose wife and son cry at his goings
and again at his return, whose lives have stopped,
waiting for him to choose.
The one who turns away now will keep walking.
A child lies down in his bed and then is a man.

Whoever cannot love today will never love,
will never make the choice a man makes,
will not build a house on a hill or a church in the woods.
Whoever is alone will stay alone a long time,
will walk through dark rooms of his house
after midnight, listening for the sounds of cars
and for the wind in the trees, and morning will not come.

DIVORCE DREAM

MARK HALLIDAY

The marriage was in a last hour of honeycombed decay,
you could tell by the moaning sound of trolleys
and the way memories had gone scaley-thin, one puff of wind
would blow marriage fragments all over the city;
I climbed the dark stairs and sprawled on the sofa,

my wife was extremely not home. The clock was loud
and busy and imperturbable in such dry air.
A phone call to my father seemed a good idea;
seemed necessary; it was the only idea.
I looked around for the phone. Things were different—

because of our being so wrong Annie and I let small things
go awry: the tail of a dead mouse stuck out
from behind a dresser and squirrels played polo
inside the walls so the house trembled
and my stomach too trembled like a dog in its sleep

and our black phone was gone. Then our landlords walked in,
our fat Irish landlords except now they were our tenants
and their children were Chinese and they all spoke
cheerfully about packages of dried noodles and puttered away
in a cloud of happy family. I should call my father—

room to room I walked behind a ribbon of shadow
emitted from a song called "I Don't Wanna Fade Away"…
All the lightbulbs were fading; on the carpet
were plops of Thanksgiving gravy; nothing mattered
compared to what mattered. Annie knew this.

Finally in her room I found the phone but it was not black
it was yellow, and it was so complicated, you had to plug it in
three different ways and wind it up and little crucial
knobs and hooks and rings kept falling loose in my hand.

INTIMACY
Kim Addonizio

℘

The woman in the café making my cappuccino—dark eyes, dyed
    red hair,
sleeveless black turtleneck—used to be lovers with the man I'm
    seeing now.
She doesn't know me; we're strangers, but still I can't glance at her
casually, as I used to, before I knew. She stands at the machine,
    sinking the nozzle
into a froth of milk, staring at nothing—I don't know what she's
    thinking.
For all I know she might be remembering my lover, remembering
    whatever happened
between them—he's never told me, except to say that it wasn't
    important, and then
he changed the subject quickly, too quickly now that I think about
    it; might he,
after all, have been lying, didn't an expression of pain cross his
    face for just
an instant? I can't be sure. And really it was nothing, I tell myself;
there's no reason for me to feel awkward standing here, or
    complicitous,
as though there's something significant between us.
She could be thinking of anything; why, now, do I have the sudden
    suspicion
that she knows, that she feels me studying her, trying to imagine
    them together?—
her lipstick's dark red, darker than her hair—trying to see him
    kissing her, turning her over in bed
the way he likes to have me. I wonder if maybe
there were things about her he preferred, things he misses now
    that we're together;
sometimes, when he and I are making love, there are moments

I'm overwhelmed by sadness, and though I'm there with him I
      can't help thinking
of my ex-husband's hands, which I especially loved, and I want to
      go back
to that old intimacy, which often felt like the purest happiness
I'd ever known, or would. But all that's over; and besides, weren't
      there other lovers
who left no trace? When I see them now, I can barely remember
what they looked like undressed, or how it felt to have them
inside me. So what is it I feel as she pours the black espresso into
      the milk,
and pushes the cup toward me, and I give her the money,
and our eyes meet for just a second, and our fingers touch?

EX-WIFE: INFATUATION

Alan Shapiro

Your voice more bashful the more intimate
it grew on that first night, an indrawn breath
of speech I can't recall beyond the miserly
sweet way it hesitated on the tongue,
chary of giving, chary of taking back,
the same breath doing both at once, it seemed,
to draw me to a closer kind of speech;

yet knowing too, knowing even then
what I—more loved than loving—had the clumsy
luxury not to know, that all too soon
what words we had to say would fail us, each
lingering syllable a syllable less
between the pleasure it held off and invited,

and the bad luck pleasure would become;
a sweet syllable closer to the other nights,
the last nights, nights that would make remembering
that long first night the bitter cost of having
had what we were on the verge of having.

BOURNEHURST-ON-THE-CANAL
GERALD COSTANZO

They arrive in the blustery
summer twilight, couples in coupes,
roadsters and touring cars, up

from Falmouth and Hyannisport
in Palm Beach suits and taffeta weave.
There is dancing to Paul Whiteman

and Alice Fay. What summons
our attention—my mother-in-law told
me this—is not the soft flags luffing

at each high corner of the pavilion,
nor the placards for photoplays screened
—during the week and after the season—

on the lower level. Not the darkened
interior, the bandstand surrounded
by potted ferns and huge portal

archways, those boxed lights
with dim figures of dancing goddesses
suspended from the iron

mesh ceiling. Never mind
that all of this will burn to the cliffside
in the autumn of 1933. Tonight it is

the one couple, vaguely familiar, lingering
by the path. They are having a quarrel—
over sex or money, because what else

could it be? Never mind that within thirty
years their eldest daughter will be
a schoolmarm in another part

of the state; that their youngest,
surely the more beautiful and promising,
will have entered into an arrangement

with the Rathbone sisters
which will be marked by sadness
and disappointment. Never mind that their

only son, a graduate of Colby College,
will live in Cleveland and embark
on a livelihood seldom

mentioned at family gatherings. Tonight
they are young, and are having
a quarrel. It is one of those evenings

full of such stirrings as only memory
will adequately "take into account." Just now
the orchestra strikes up and music

floats over the distance to where they are
being a little brusque with each other,
a little stubborn.

And now, as if called, they begin to move
toward the ballroom entrance, he slightly ahead
and tugging at her wrist, though not quite

so much to cause pain.
He believes the moment has passed
and he is leading her toward

an evening of happiness.
Toward a lifetime
of happiness.

WHEN A WOMAN LOVES A MAN
DAVID LEHMAN

When she says margarita she means daiquiri.
When she says *quixotic* she means *mercurial*.
And when she says, "I'll never speak to you again,"
she means, "Put your arms around me from behind
as I stand disconsolate at the window."

He's supposed to know that.

When a man loves a woman he is in New York and she is in Virginia
or he is in Boston, writing, and she is in New York, reading,
or she is wearing a sweater and sunglasses in Balboa Park and he
        is raking the leaves in Ithaca
or he is driving to East Hampton and she is standing disconsolate
        at the window overlooking the bay
where a regatta of many-colored sails is going on
while he is stuck in traffic on the Long Island Expressway.

When a woman loves a man it is one ten in the morning
she is asleep he is watching the ball scores and eating pretzels
drinking lemonade
and two hours later he wakes up and staggers into bed
where she remains asleep and very warm.

When she says tomorrow she means in three or four weeks.
When she says, "We're talking about me now,"
he stops talking. Her best friend comes over and says,
"Did somebody die?"

When a woman loves a man, they have gone
to swim naked in the stream
on a glorious July day

with the sound of the waterfall like a chuckle
of water rushing over smooth rocks,
and there is nothing alien in the universe.

Ripe apples fall about them.
What else can they do but eat?

When he says, "Ours is a transitional era,"
"that's very original of you," she replies,
dry as the martini he is sipping.

They fight all the time
It's fun
What do I owe you?
Let's start with an apology
OK, I'm sorry, you dickhead.
A sign is held up saying "Laughter."
It's a silent picture.
"I've been fucked without a kiss," she says,
"and you can quote me on that,"
which sounds great in an English accent.

One year they broke up seven times and threatened to do it
        another nine times.

When a woman loves a man, she wants him to meet her at the
        airport in a foreign country with a jeep.
When a man loves a woman he's there. He doesn't complain that
        she's two hours late
and there's nothing in the refrigerator.

When a woman loves a man, she wants to stay awake.
She's like a child crying
at nightfall because she didn't want the day to end.

When a man loves a woman, he watches her sleep, thinking:
as midnight to the moon, is sleep to the beloved.
A thousand fireflies wink at him.
The frogs sound like the string section
of the orchestra warming up.
The stars dangle down like earrings the shape of grapes.

INTIMATIONS OF INFIDELITY
Cynthia Huntington

Sometimes a headache is just a headache;
other times it might be brain cancer.

As the mobster's mother said, "You die
in your own arms." You believe in life

without purpose, you try to live by will and
manic reason, you end up talking to your horse,

like Nietzsche. Nietzsche is dead.
The horse died also, after great suffering.

It was an inflammation of the brain, a mental
combustion, fever of hope run riot.

I sensed a great disturbance in the house.
I felt cancer in my brain. It was an earwig

that bored into my skull and whispered
to my frontal lobes my loving husband

had been screwing everything that moved.
One in particular I suspect

was not even moving. The clock is ticking.
Pay attention; it might be a bomb.

Sometimes a pressure in your chest
will wake you in the middle of the night,

squeezing your lungs, a fire climbing
up your throat. You sit up, choking for breath.

It might be a bad dream, or something you ate.
Another time, it's a heart attack.

CROSS-COUNTRY
PETER COVINO

Before my sister's divorce, I imagined driving her
back to her previous life, across Nevada, Arizona…

stopping alongside a dirt road near San Antonio,
on the way to the Mannerist Art Exhibition.

Because I want a redemptive art:
Pontormo's *Deposition* in Santa Felicità.

Because I understand how the Menendez brothers
must have felt, bullet holes of redemption;

and Susan Smith who made sure her boys
were securely strapped in seat belts before she drowned them—

Our own mother *would have eaten us at birth*
had she known how we'd turn out.

Give me Daniele da Volterra's *Crucifixion*,
anything by Bronzino, or Vasari—

I phoned my oldest sister this evening, the one father
couldn't get at when he lived away from us in Venezuela.

I wanted to tell her how this divorce was not news to me:
this was a clear case, with an antecedent.

I wanted to tell her clearly,
because we cannot always tell clearly.

I wanted to make her understand.
Because it's love we want.

WALKING HOME ACROSS THE ISLAND
JACK GILBERT

Walking home across the plain in the dark.
And Linda crying. Again we have come
to a place where I rail and she suffers and the moon
does not rise. We have only each other,
but I am shouting inside the rain
and she is crying like a wounded animal,
knowing there is no place to turn. It is hard
to understand how we could be brought here by love.

THE NIGHT BEFORE LEAVING

LINDA GREGG

We sit at the kitchen table
waiting for some opening.
For the proper handling
of goodbye.
Going deeper and deeper
into the hours, like slow divers
sinking in their heavy gear.
We look at each other, gesturing
which way to go
through the lamplight,
garbage bags, dishes in the sink
and on the table.
We surface in a kind of dream.
The boat touches ground.
Grinds onto the rocks.
We get out,
and it floats again.

SELF-IMPROVEMENT
TONY HOAGLAND

Just before she flew off like a swan
to her wealthy parents' summer home,
Bruce's college girlfriend asked him
to improve his expertise at oral sex,
and offered him some technical advice:

Use nothing but his tonguetip
to flick the light switch in his room
on and off a hundred times a day
until he grew fluent at the nuances
of force and latitude.

Imagine him at practice every evening,
more inspired than he ever was at algebra,
beads of sweat sprouting on his brow,
thinking, *thirty-seven*, *thirty-eight*,
seeing, in the tunnel vision of his mind's eye,
the quadratic equation of her climax
yield to the logic
of his simple math.

Maybe he unscrewed
the bulb from his apartment ceiling
so that passersby would not believe
a giant firefly was pulsing
its electric abdomen in 13 B.

Maybe, as he stood
two inches from the wall,
in darkness, fogging the old plaster
with his breath, he visualized the future

as a mansion standing on the shore
that he was rowing to
with his tongue's exhausted oar.

Of course, the girlfriend dumped him:
met someone, après-ski, who,
using nothing but his nose
could identify the vintage of a Cabernet.

Sometimes we are asked
to get good at something we have
no talent for,
or we excel at something we will never
have the opportunity to prove.

Often we ask ourselves
to make absolute sense
out of what just happens,
and in this way, what we are practicing

is suffering,
which everybody practices,
but strangely few of us
grow graceful in.

The climaxes of suffering are complex,
costly, beautiful, but secret.
Bruce never played the light switch again.

So the avenues we walk down,
full of bodies wearing faces,
are full of hidden talent:
enough to make pianos moan,
sidewalks split,
streetlights deliriously flicker.

DEEP RIVER MOTOR INN

CYNTHIA HUNTINGTON

No depth there for dreaming.
All night the roar of trucks
beneath your window, their hum and grind
like a river's current, carries you down,
dragged over rocks and sand,
turning headlong, spun into its rush.

You lie on the white bed,
on cool sheets, turning;
the traffic surges below,
and all night you are traveling,
borne down in its rush.
Your penis curls limp against you,

a drop of blood on the tip.
Stain of semen, scent of cunt
on your fingers, strange liquor
in your hair, that alien touch.
If you could sleep, if you could sink
down here, rest and begin dreaming,

this time you could make it real.
Lights sweep the ceiling and are gone.
Like the pressure of an unfamiliar kiss—
the river that has carried you
out of your life, away from your home,
lost, no country here your own.

AFTER SUMMER FELL APART

YUSEF KOMUNYAKAA

I can't touch you.
His face always returns;
we exchange long looks
in each bad dream
& what I see, my God.
Honey, sweetheart,
I hold you against me
but nothing works.
Two boats moored,
rocking between nowhere
& nowhere.
A bone inside me whispers
maybe tonight,
but I keep thinking
about the two men wrestling nude
in Lawrence's *Women in Love.*
I can't get past
reels of breath unwinding.
He has you. Now
he doesn't. He has you
again. Now he doesn't.
You're at the edge of azaleas
shaken loose by a word.
I see your rose-colored
skirt unfurl.
He has a knife
to your throat,
night birds come back
to their branches.
A hard wind raps at the door,
the new year prowling

in a black overcoat.
It's been six months
since we made love.
Tonight I look at you
hugging the pillow,
half smiling in your sleep.
I want to shake you & ask
who. Again I touch myself,
unashamed, until
his face comes into focus.
He's stolen something
from me & I don't know
if it has a name or not—
like counting your ribs
with one foolish hand
& mine with the other.

HOME TOGETHER
RAVI SHANKAR

Between us the vacuum of early evening,
A pot of rice and beans simmering on the stove.
Between us, for now, an easy domesticity,
The way we move past each other without words,
A thin breeze hitched up to bay windows,
Our footsteps rattling on the hardwood floors.
Words are there though, invisible yet sharp
As incisors pulled from a hound's drooling jaw,
Words we can never have meant to speak,
But did, recanted, then spoke again.
Such words should have died in our lungs.
They have staked between us a fence of teeth.

*Mostly true
or one-sidedly true?*

EX-WIFE: HOMESICKNESS
Alan Shapiro

Voice that would wake me
in the bland American
too anywhereness
of the rented room we lived in,—
on those last nights
together when realizing
you would soon leave
seemed to revive so
cruelly our earliest delights
in one another;

voice not meant for my ears,
risen, it seemed, from some
never before sounded
privacy within you,
permitting you to hear—
as you murmured that
you wanted to go home
to Ireland, home, home,—
how the word you thought
would speak only your longing

now spoke grief, spoke
dread, and not for me,
or us, or anything
at all you'd leave behind,
but for the very thing
you wanted to go home to,
everything you'd find
before the hearth fire,
drink in hand, sheer
animal solace in the sound

of wind and slant rain
at the gabled window,
against the roof and walls,
the room all lair, all burrow,
and you within it safer
for the storm's familiar
harrowing that kept
your need to be at home
there, always,
not inordinate.

REUNIONS WITH A GHOST
AI

The first night God created was too weak;
it fell down on its back,
a woman in a cobalt blue dress.
I was that woman and I didn't die.
I lived for you,
but you don't care. You're drunk again,
turned inward as always.
Nobody has trouble like I do, you tell me,
unzipping your pants
to show me the scar on your thigh,
where the train sliced into you
when you were ten.
You talk about it with wonder and self-contempt,
because you didn't die
and you think you deserved to.
When I kneel to touch it,
you just stand there
with your eyes closed,
your pants and underwear bunched at your ankles.
I slide my hand up your thigh
to the scar and you shiver
and grab me by the hair.
We kiss, we sink to the floor,
but we never touch it,
we just go on and on tumbling through space
like two bits of stardust that shed no light,
until it's finished,
our descent, our falling in place.
We sit up. Nothing's different, nothing.
Is it love, is it friendship
that pins us down,

until we give in,
then rise defeated once more
to reenter the sanctuary of our separate lives?
Sober now, you dress,
then sit watching me
go through the motions of reconstruction—
reddening cheeks, eyeshadowing eyelids,
sticking bobby pins here and there.
We kiss outside
and you walk off, arm in arm with your demon.
So I've come through the ordeal of loving once again,
sane, whole, wise, I think as I watch you,
and when you turn back, I see in your eyes
acceptance, resignation,
certainty that we must collide from time to time.
Yes. Yes, I meant goodbye when I said it.

for Jim

CODA
James Tate

Love is not worth so much;
I regret everything.
Now on our backs
in Fayetteville, Arkansas,
the stars are falling
into our cracked eyes.

With my good arm
I reach for the sky,
and let the air out of the moon.
It goes whizzing off
to shrivel and sink
in the ocean.

You cannot weep;
I cannot do anything
that once held an ounce
of meaning for us.
I cover you
with pine needles.

When morning comes,
I will build a cathedral
around our bodies.
And the crickets,
who sing with their knees,
will come there
in the night to be sad,
when they can sing no more.

TERRIBLE LOVE
Kevin Prufer

Wish the lights would go back on, wish it was spring already.
Wish the bees would fly back home from my living room.
Hear them singing and horsing around in there? Rattle, rattle
against the porcelain, fire screen, window panes, their unfeeble buzz
rising to racket-level till one by one the portraits fall from the walls.
They enjoy the glow the space heater provides.

When we moved in here—my young wife and I—the place was merely
tumble-down: chips in the walls, blackened floors, and leaves spreading,
        fan-like,
from the cracks beneath the doors. We unloaded the bed first.
I said, "We'll consummate things here—and here, and here," pointing
first to that bed, and then to the leafswept places. She stood in the kitchen
unloading the flatware. One by one, her forks tumbled to the floor.

I was terribly in love, but it wasn't long
before she shuddered at my breath on her neck. She is a woman
of great distractions and hairpins. I swept the leaves from the doorways
and her laughs came as blackish clouds, her words snowdots or beetles,
        depending.
Sometimes I wouldn't see her all day, so busy was she
singing to herself in the gardens behind the house. I swept and swept,
cleaned the pipes, caulked the walls as best I could.

Then it was November and the ice thickened
in invisible leaks in the bricks. When the winds came, the trees shook
their twig-tips until the windows cracked. The bees arrived later,
sensing, somehow, the house an escape from the cold.
Wish they were gone. Wish I had something to clot the walls.
My wife, in her bedrobe, drew an invisible line
at the foot of the stairs. "Here is for you," she told me, sweeping

the downstairs with her hand. Now she lives in the master chamber
at the top of the stairs. All day, behind the bees, I hear
ice cracking in those leaky veins. The bricks fall, startlingly,
into the yard. Sometimes I hear her slippers skipping over my head.
She sings to herself and moves the bed around. Is she tying
a great escape from the bed sheets? Does she scale
the rose trellises at night? And for whom? My poor skin

is brailled over with stings. I wish the spring storms would come.
Wish the gardens would bloom, thorn over the path to the road.
Wish there was something I could say.

GIVING MYSELF UP

MARK STRAND

I give up my eyes which are glass eggs.
I give up my tongue.
I give up my mouth which is the constant dream of my
       tongue.
I give up my throat which is the sleeve of my voice.
I give up my heart which is a burning apple.
I give up my lungs which are trees that have never seen
       the moon.
I give up my smell which is that of a stone traveling
       through rain.
I give up my hands which are ten wishes.
I give up my arms which have wanted to leave me anyway.
I give up my legs which are lovers only at night.
I give up my buttocks which are the moons of childhood.
I give up my penis which whispers encouragement to my
       thighs.
I give up my clothes which are walls that blow in the wind
and I give up the ghost that lives in them.
I give up. I give up.
And you will have none of it because already I am beginning
again without anything.

II

In the Middle of the Storm

LISTENER
Stephen Berg

he heard the phone
he picked up the receiver
he said hello
he took off his glasses
he moved a letter on his desk
he heard her say and not say
he asked he asked again
he knew her words weren't the real words
he joked
he had that old wish for God a signpost
he needed it but it was all weakness
he even heard a biblical sigh wisdom icons
he could feel the storm of pain approaching
he asked anyhow
he heard the other one's grieving facts
he could do nothing except talk
he advised he soothed he did all that
he listened
he heard every syllable there was
he thought troops were marching upstairs in a house in a fallen
       country
he heard birds at the same time
he understood there could be birds and desolation
he knew this was a lesson he resisted always
he blessed the victims of bad luck
he blessed the victims of good luck
he wanted to tear out someone's eyes someone who deserved all that
       happens

SLOWLY

DONNA MASINI

I watched a snake once, swallow a rabbit.
Fourth grade, the reptile zoo
the rabbit stiff, nose in, bits of litter stuck to its fur,

its head clenched in the wide
jaws of the snake, the snake
sucking it down its long throat.

All throat that snake—I couldn't tell
where the throat ended, the body
began. I remember the glass

case, the way that snake
took its time (all the girls, groaning, shrieking
but weren't we amazed, fascinated,

saying we couldn't look, but looking, weren't we
held there, weren't we
imagining—what were we imagining?).

Mrs. Peterson urged us to *move on girls*,
but we couldn't move. It was like
watching a fern unfurl, a minute

hand move across a clock. I didn't know why
the snake didn't choke, the rabbit never
moved, how the jaws kept opening

wider, sucking it down, just so
I am taking this in, slowly,
taking it into my body:

this grief. How slow
the body is to realize.
You are never coming back.

ADAM AND EVE
Tony Hoagland

I wanted to punch her right in the mouth and that's the truth.

After all, we had gotten from the station of the flickering glances
to the station of the hungry mouths,
from the shoreline of skirts and faded jeans
to the ocean of unencumbered skin,
from the perilous mountaintop of the apartment steps
to the sanctified valley of the bed—

the candle fluttering upon the dresser top, its little yellow blade
sending up its whiff of waxy smoke,
and I could smell her readiness
like a dank cloud above a field,

when at the crucial moment, the all-important moment,
the moment standing at attention,

she held her milk white hand agitatedly
over the entrance to her body and said *No*,

and my brain burst into flame.

If I couldn't sink myself in her like a dark spur
or dissolve into her like a clod thrown in a river,

can I go all the way in the saying, and say
I wanted to punch her right in the face?
Am I allowed to say that,
that I wanted to punch her right in her soft face?

Or is the saying just another instance of rapaciousness,
just another way of doing what I wanted then,
by saying it?

Is a man just an animal, and is a woman not an animal?
Is the name of the animal power?
Is it true that the man wishes to see the woman
hurt with her own pleasure

and the woman wishes to see the expression on the man's face
of someone falling from great height,
that the woman thrills with the power of her weakness
and the man is astonished by the weakness of his power?

Is the sexual chase a hunt where the animal inside
drags the human down
into a jungle made of vowels,
hormonal undergrowth of sweat and hair,

or is this an obsolete idea
lodged like a fossil
in the brain of the ape
who lives inside the man?

Can the fossil be surgically removed
or dissolved, or redesigned
so the man can be a human being, like a woman?

Does the woman see the man as a house
where she might live in safety,
and does the man see the woman as a door
through which he might escape
the hated prison of himself,

and when the door is locked,
does he hate the door instead?
Does he learn to hate all doors?

I've seen rain turn into snow then back to rain,
and I've seen making love turn into fucking
then back to making love,
and no one covered up their faces out of shame,
no one rose and walked into the lonely maw of night.

But where was there, in fact, to go?
Are some things better left unsaid?
Shall I tell you her name?
Can I say it again,
that I wanted to punch her right in the face?

Until we say the truth, there can be no tenderness.
As long as there is desire, we will not be safe.

FINISHED

Aɪ

You force me to touch
the black, rubber flaps
of the garbage disposal
that is open like a mouth saying, ah.
You tell me it's the last thing I'll feel
before I go numb.
Is it my screaming that finally stops you,
or is it the fear
that even you are too near the edge
of this Niagara to come back from?
You jerk my hand out
and give me just enough room
to stagger around you.
I lean against the refrigerator,
not looking at you, or anything,
just staring at a space which you no longer inhabit,
that you've abandoned completely now
to footsteps receding
to the next feeding station,
where a woman will be eaten alive
after cocktails at five.
The flowers and chocolates, the kisses,
the swings and near misses of new love
will confuse her,
until you start to abuse her,
verbally at first.
As if trying to quench a thirst,
You'll drink her
in small outbursts of rage
then you'll whip out your semiautomatic,
make her undress, or listen to hours

of radio static as torture
for being amazed that the man of her dreams
is a nightmare, who only seems happy
when he's making her suffer.

The first time you hit me,
I left you, remember?
It was December. An icy rain was falling
and it froze on the roads,
so that driving was unsafe, but not as unsafe
as staying with you.
I ran outside in my nightgown,
while you yelled at me to come back.
When you came after me,
I was locked in the car.
You smashed the window with a crowbar,
but I drove off anyway.
I was back the next day
and we were on the bare mattress,
because you'd ripped up the sheets,
saying you'd teach me a lesson.
You wouldn't speak except
to tell me I needed discipline,
needed training in the fine art
of remaining still
when your fist slammed into my jaw.
You taught me how ropes could be tied
so I'd strangle myself,
how pressure could be applied to old wounds
until I cried for mercy,
until tonight, when those years
of our double exposure end
with shot after shot.

How strange it is to be unafraid.
When the police come,

I'm sitting at the table,
the cup of coffee
that I am unable to drink
as cold as your body.
I shot him, I say, he beat me.
I do not tell them how the emancipation from pain
leaves nothing in its place.

MINNEAPOLIS
Patricia Smith

Ouch. The first hurt is when I see you
standing in the lobby of my hotel, pacing,
hands shoved deep in your pockets. All
nervous blinks and questions. I realize then
that it is already too late, that common sense
is no friend of ours, and I consider saying
"I have fallen in love with you" and
touching the flat of my hand against your
grizzled cheek, just to see whether you would
run, or weep. The wine, of course, is desperate
ritual, a last chance to laugh it off and return,
shaky and solemn, to the clutches of home.
We sip and giggle, our eyes jumping,
and I hungry-stare at your left hand resting
on the table, wondering if it has memorized me.

Ouch. But I am in your arms, pressed against
the door of my room, drinking in all this wrong,
biting and kissing, clutching, but this is not home,
this is not home, this is breath, this is downbeat,
this, oh my God, forgive me, this is my latest
religion. I fold myself under you, pass through
your skin, introduce my anxious tongues
to the swell of your belly, fill my fists
with soft steel-colored curls. And our kisses
are dirge rhythm then jazz quick, strutting
like bullies on the bass line of us.
My whole body is hurt, then hallelujah,
hurt, then hallelujah again,
regretting then reveling in this deception.
Somewhere it says thou shall not commit this.

The last thing I want is this stranger inside me.
The next thing I want is this stranger inside me.
The only thing I want is this stranger inside me.
The only thing I want is this stranger.
There are too many of us in this one room. Your wife
stands cool and detached by the window, my husband
sits on the side of the bed with his head in his hands.
We weep and fuck, so sweet slowly, so flustered and
needing, forgetting to eat or drink, ignoring the screams
from our respective corners. That nagging question,
"What are we doing?" is answered a million and one
times because it is what we *keep* doing, *ouch,* it is what
we can't stop doing, shattering our lives and dancing
barefoot on the shards of glass. When I say I love you
it is the first poem I ever wrote, and when you answer
I love you too, it is the sound that poem makes in the open air.

Ouch. At the sight of us, your wife moans regret.
My husband stops his tears long enough to ask me
how I could do this. I twist my body into goodbye,
squeeze my eyes shut against the sight of you.
Your plane home guns its engines
just outside the window.

THE STORY
GERALD COSTANZO

For years I tried
to write the story called
"Excavating the Ruins of Miami
Beach." I guess I needed
to give some meaning
to that time after the divorce
when my life, all alcohol
and remorse, moved at a pace
far slower than I could adapt
to; one of those times when living
becomes a cruel parody
of our intention.

After ten months,
we were back together—
for who knows what reasons.
We could not live with each other,
then couldn't successfully
live apart. Still there was bitterness.
The accusations. Even deceit. Everything
wreckage and impossibility.

It was the summer we took
our children on that loopy
odyssey across the South
just to avoid the place where trouble
was—at least the part of it
that wasn't us. I think now
we were lucky to live in a country

where you can become someone
else so easily.

★   ★   ★

At the south end of Miami Beach,
just off Collins Ave., beyond
the beautiful seedy tropical Deco hotels
and beside the Adler Burlesque,
years out of its time, the sidewalk
sandwich-board proclaiming *Songstress
Claire Barry of the Famous 'Barry Sisters'
and Hilarious Comedian Larry Best
with his Apple Routine—Next Week:
the Vibrant Voice of the Lovely Helen
Marr*, was a lunch counter named Big
Daddy's. I walked in,
my four-year-old son on my hand,
and there were the photographs
that made the minute-to-minute
I was living seem less immediate, less
full of consequence, again.
On the walls hundreds of group portraits
of the proprietor and his family alongside
celebrities, all their names stamped out
in tape-gun plastic and affixed
to the frames: Big Daddy, Mrs. Big Daddy,
and the kid—Big Daddy Jr., posed among
Tiny Tim, Johnny Weismuller, Henny
Youngman, Roland La Starza, Troy
Donohue, and Dr. Joyce Brothers.

My son at his meal, I roved
the mystical gallery: Myron Cohen, Fabian,
Jack E. Leonard, Frank Sinatra Jr.,
Patty Duke, and Jose Ferrer. I remember
dreaming, in this land of lunch hour
patrons and the adult incarnation

of Big Daddy Jr. teaching two Vietnamese
boys to wipe down a table, that I
was an archaeologist. I remember laughing.

★ ★ ★

I couldn't write
the story, though I lived in it
for a while and was myself
occupied.
    Walking out, my son
eager for his own next episode,
I understood from the curious half-hour
that—hard as I tried—I couldn't solve
any of my problems; and that this,
finally, was how I'd begun
to outgrow them.

THE PURE LONELINESS
Michael Ryan

Late at night, when you're so lonely,
your shoulders curl toward the center of your body,
you call no one and you don't call out.

This is dignity. This is the pure loneliness
that made Christ think he was God.
This is why lunatics smile at their thoughts.

Even the best moment, as you slip
half-a-foot deep into someone you like,
sinks through the loneliness in it
to the loneliness that's not.

If you believe in Christ hanging on the cross,
his arms spread as if to embrace
the Father he calls who is somewhere else,

you still might hear your own voice
at your next great embrace, thinking
loneliness in another can't be touched,

like Christ's voice at death answering Himself.

SONG OF AN X

BETH GYLYS

Don't think of me
as you pull
shirts out of the washer,
or wipe the chocolate
from your child's face.
Don't think of me
bathing, or slipping
from my dress.
Don't imagine my bare shoulders,
my hair hanging loose
as I dance through empty rooms.
Don't stop to think of me
as you take the hand
of your wife across the table.
Don't think of my thoughts,
my laughter, my umbrella,
my tongue, my tall black boots,
my way of sighing.
Don't think of me lonely,
or making love,
or lit darkly by candles,
as you step outside
to retrieve the morning paper,
dressed only in your bathrobe
and a pair of old gray socks.
Don't think of me.

THEIR DIVORCE
Stephen Dunn

Not them. Not even with the best
binoculars on the bluest day
could I have seen it coming.
Not with scrutiny's microscope,
or with the help of history or gossip.
Of all people, not them.
They hadn't fallen in love with others.
Not even a night of drink
or proximity's slow burn drove them
to lapse, say, with a coworker.
It means no one can know what goes on
in the pale trappings of bedrooms,
in anyone's secret, harrowed heart.
It makes time itself an executioner—
a fact I always knew
applied to couples
whose bodies contradicted
their Darling this, Honey that,
and even some who exhibited
true decency and respect.
But this is a mockery, a defeat.
My friends were perfect, *perfect*.
"Every married couple appearing together
in public is comic," Adorno said,
and I wrote "Stupid!" in the margin.
Now they're broken up, finished.
Oh Adorno, you son of a bitch,
you perspicacious bastard,
sometimes what a cold eye sees
lasts longer than any of us.

THE MONARCHS: 44
ALISON HAWTHORNE DEMING

Night. A woman betrayed.
Insects gather
on the cabin window
so that all she can see
is a plague of gray moths.
She's sick of the body's
dumb song, the frenzy
of insects for light.
Why does a moth do that
if it's nocturnal?
If it woke up in the daytime,
it could simply
have what it wants.

THE SPORTING LIFE
BOB HICOK

He and his wife have split.
As an atom does when violently asked, when struck by a hammer
           of some kind.
Release of energy sounds so polite, a bird of lightning
           shown an open cage, a hurricane
           issued a passport.
An hurricane, yes.
There are standards, I see that.
An hurricane in the shape of my friend is nine-ironing beer bottles
           off the roof of his apartment.
That's what he said he was going to do, his chin a smaller roof,
           me on the opposite side of his car, eyes closed,
           listening to his moon-dust voice,
           voice of being two hundred and fifty thousand miles away.
Twenty years since someone told me, mine are not the toes for her,
           not the bad breath of her dreams.
As if a saw—band or circular, your hardware, your choice—
           cut through my shins and again just above the knees, a section
           removed, one critical to standing, one certain to be noticed
           in an inventory.
I've learned this much: empathy is shit.
Not to bother telling him, I've been there, as if being told to go away
           is a place, magazines on cheap tables, mug shots of open sores
           on the walls, a plant flowering eye teeth in the corner,
           a window overlooking a trade school for maggots.
I get to kiss my wife any time her lips aren't in another state,
           they've been in Washington, Michigan, New York, her lips
           would like to visit all fifty states by the time it's over,
           visit Greece, birth place of western lips, visit Paris,
           City of Lips.

I could feel the wind before he left, knew his arms and legs, his hair,
        were spinning around a center where nothing is felt, dead place
        where the only sound is the word hello ripped on the head of a
nail
        poised above a knee cap, there's a child, you see, sound of daddy
        on the telephone, the coffin click of goodbye.
We're poorly designed.
Too porous, too prone to flesh, we should be, not the wire
        but what thrives in the wire, just hum, flow, all together
        in a soup of plasma, fuck the differentiated self, the cliché
        of identity, here's to vanishing, to forgiving a man
        shouting four before a rain shower of brown glass.
It could be, was you, is me, we all go boom, just wait, so what
        exactly.
Which leaves only his swing to discuss, choice of clubs, those silly shoes
        golfers wear, the ones with spikes in the bottom, like they're at
war
        with grass.

DANCER HOLDING STILL

LINDA GREGG

Her husband has left and no man moves her.
A breeze might turn her face so the hair
would hang long behind her shoulders,
but no man does. She stands because her body
wants to stand. She sits for the same reason.
She sleeps on her side in the night. Years
of dark, with stars sometimes, sometimes with
summer fire in the grass. She is not waiting.
She keeps from knowing the grief of separation.
She thinks the love will not kill her. His love
is powerful in her, the way metal loves heat.

SEPARATED FATHER

MARK HALLIDAY

Driving along the city's edge at night
he obeys all traffic signals with chilly prudence.
God might be watching for an excuse to nail him.
He has ceased to live in the house where his daughter lives.
What could be more wrong?
Yet the car is running smoothly; it doesn't know
what kind of man is at the wheel. Indeed
most people seem unable to read on his face
what he has done. Lone cowboy of the night
beyond civilization, he feels ice-gloved
in the unmistakable primacy of self,
who used to think he'd do anything
for his little girl. When he drives past the house
at 2 A.M., slowly, to see her dark window
and believe she is sleeping soundly, he recognizes himself
as protagonist of more than one rather dreary short story
but now it's him,
       it's him
and the moon is so bright:
above his car and later above his tiny new apartment
it is so damned
bright that no one (not his wife, not any smart or wise person)
can tell him it isn't romantic. Unfortunately
it is romantic. So
he has a new phone, and he has one mint wrapped in silver
from a restaurant called La Famiglia, where no one knew he was a dad;
and he'll phone the woman who changed the meaning of joy.

FUCK YOU POEM #45

AMY GERSTLER

✍

Fuck you in slang and conventional English.
Fuck you in lost and neglected lingoes.
Fuck you hungry and sated; faded, pock-marked and
defaced.
Fuck you with orange rind, fennel and anchovy paste.
Fuck you with rosemary and thyme, and fried green olives
on the side.
Fuck you humidly and icily.
Fuck you farsightedly and blindly.
Fuck you nude and draped in stolen finery.
Fuck you while cells divide wildly and birds trill.
Thank you for barring me from his bedside while he was ill.
Fuck you puce and chartreuse.
Fuck you postmodern and prehistoric.
Fuck you under the influence of opium, codeine, laudanum
and paregoric.
Fuck every real and imagined country you fancied yourself
princess of.
Fuck you on feast days and fast days, below and above.
Fuck you sleepless and shaking for nineteen nights
running.
Fuck you ugly and fuck you stunning.
Fuck you shipwrecked on the barren island of your bed.
Fuck you marching in lockstep in the ranks of the dead.
Fuck you at low and high tide.
And fuck you astride
                           anyone who has the bad luck to fuck
you, in dank hallways,
          bathrooms, or kitchens.
Fuck you in gasps and whispered benedictions.

And fuck these curses, however heartfelt and true,
that bind me, till I forgive you, to you.

SO LONG LONELY AVENUE

JAMES HARMS

> "In this case I think it's better to face it—we belong together."
> — RICKIE LEE JONES

I remember Lani floating from her body
and asking me to ask the surgeon for her teeth.
And how she sang over and over
"We belong together," while I carried her
to the car and folded her in, slipped a prescription
in her blouse and put her hand there, as if
pledging her allegiance, or holding her heart in.
We drove across Bloomington,
the spring air thick as a thousand feet of water.
Lani sang in her seat at a stop light as a boy
in a blue Chevy watched and frowned,
his idle erasing her song. Her head
lolled back like a child's beneath a night sky—
stars for the begging, the moon
dripping into a pail of old rainwater.
She kept singing, "We belong together."
I carried her up the stairs to bed and brought her
soup and straws to sip it through,
I brushed her hair one hundred times.
A week later, with cheeks like Dizzy Gillespie
and codeine in her veins,
Lani searched all day for cilantro
and made salsa in the middle of Indiana.
We trimmed our three rooms
with white, red and green, and invited everyone
we sort of liked to our place
for Cinco de Mayo. It was a night where
people fell down a great deal.

All year we'd looked for that apartment,
where she could work and I could work
and we could throw parties and be better forever.
But that was a small, wound-up idea
of how two people come into each other's arms
repeatedly for the time it takes to
ask for everything, and to take what's given.
Then, one day, he asks for something
she doesn't have, something she's never had,
and he asks because he knows this, that
she can't give anymore. So he leaves.

THROUGH THE GLASS

Beth Gylys

As usual, you're in your office on the phone.
But when you see me coming, you shut your door
so I can't hear. Your latest news: another
wants you; you say that it's complex. You want
to keep things sane, to stay alone, married.
You're worried you might hurt us all. Of course.

You didn't have to tell me. I've felt you pulling
away as if we were attached. I watch you
through the glass; you're flushed, nervous with me
waiting here, though you talk as if I weren't
sitting at your door, my hands numb,
shaking with pain. How can we stop ourselves

from wanting? Do I touch you with my eyes?
You have a wife, me, and now this third;
we rotate around you like three human moons.
You turn; your hand is raised. What should I think?
What should I feel? I'd like to say it doesn't
matter. Should I lie to spare myself?

You act surprised when you come out: "Are you
okay? What's wrong?" as if it's nothing, nothing:
Why am I upset? You aren't so honest
after all, and I a moon whose face
is bruised with shade. I'll shine my harvest smile:
I'm fine, complicit in my sorry way.

Having felt your hands on fire with years
of longing, having felt my own hot fire
emerge to meet you, finally, finally, I'm bound
to you—we all are—held in our own ways.
You will love your women as you like,
and I will eat myself like homemade bread.

5:14 FROM CHICAGO

Bob Hicok

A friend comes from out of town.
His wife left him to live alone in a loft with books.
His Marley t-shirt isn't prepared for December,
and he smells like whiskey at thirty-five thousand feet.
His eyes are burning in the puddle of his face.
The bag he forgot at home is probably empty.
He says *hi* like the last air out of a tire.
I show him the windmill on the way from the airport,
   the blades are cotton and white, they are angels
   spinning.
I neglect to point at the trailer in which a man
   hung his wife and baby and shot himself
   in the groin to confess and bleed out.
Three deer jump in front of us across the road,
emphasizing the weightless parts of existence.
He touches my wife's hand hello beside a Catawba tree.
The fire in the fireplace is talking to itself.
He falls asleep and twitches in a black chair
   like a shot animal not yet convinced
   of the bullet.
Two hours later, he comes into the kitchen
   wearing the slept-in bed of his face.
My wife is cutting carrots and peppers and onions,
her hands as fast as an auction.
I put on music which is safely out of words, out of love
   and missing and needing back.
He sets the table and gives himself three spoons.
Salad, bread, pasta, green beans.
He touches the lettuce with a spoon as if to reassure it
   his indifference isn't personal,
and I feel the hole of him growing.

He says his wife's name by stroking the soft wood
        of the table.
The nine o'clock windows surrounding us are mirrors.
With seven days of beard, I resemble forgetting.
My wife goes to bed.
He picks up her napkin and tells me I'm lucky,
but I remember falling to the floor when a woman left me,
        how good it felt, cool and staying down there
        for three years.
When the wine's gone he switches to vodka.
He makes it outside in time to get on his knees and throw up
        as snow halos his face.
Snow makes it feel like the world is trying as hard as it can
        to listen.
We sit, wet-assed and shivering.
He screams and of course the mountains say *so what*.
What I like about the air is it heals as you crack it open.
He makes a snow angel so I do to keep his company.
In minutes, snow fills our angels like heaven wants them back.
I look at the smoke of his breath, this is what burning down,
        what *fuck it* looks like.
He takes off his ring and swallows it.
Tomorrow, he'll search his shit for gold.

BREAKDOWN
PATRICIA SMITH

You've gone crazy. I've packed everything I am
to come to you. Your eyes are rolling back into
your head, your heart is rolling back into history,
your words are rolling away from me. You make
me read a letter you wrote to your wife. You won't
stop crying. You come home from work, and I see
the madness in you. You walk in circles, sweat
dots the front of your shirt. I think you are full
of shit. I think you are full of longing. I unpack
boxes in my head. I write you a letter that begins
with *I love you* and ends with *I love you* and
somewhere in the middle is one goodbye for
every hurt. I run out of time, I run out of paper,
I run out of steam. The key for the letter G and
the key for the letter O and the key for the letter D
and the key for the letter B and the key for the letter
Y and the key for the letter E fly off my keyboard,
they are tired, as tired as I am of the pushpull that is
this crazy you, this out of control, careening you,
this you who comes home and says *I have made
an appointment to talk to someone.* Talk to me,
talk to me, talk to me for free, tell me how inside
out you are, tell me how you can be the same man
whose kisses twisted me away from this world,
tell me what "I am in love with two women" means,
instruct me in the fine art of unpacking boxes.
Let loose those bottles of Gentleman Jack,
stop thirsting for things that are bitter,
go crazy here, here in these arms that are still
wrapped around the absent shape of you,
go crazy with me, thrash about in our bed

and weep and wail and call me by her name,
at least have the courage to let our hearts break together,
here in this place where I can reach down,
grab a shard and cut my fuckin' throat.

YOU
DENIS JOHNSON

You were as blind to me
as your footprints last Friday,
but I saw you dancing
with that girl who wasn't me—
because I don't dance
and laugh in that terrible
style with every stranger.
But you are no stranger.

But you were strange when you were dancing,
and the room turned all yellow
and the glass I was holding
spilled burgundy wine.
I got out by the side door
and I leaned on a box,
and I saw you at the end
of every street,

and in the Flame Inn
I watched the men shooting
eight-ball and mule-kicking
the jukebox till it worked.
On the wall they had many,
many wooden plaques
bearing humorous sayings
that I will never say
to you even if you begged me,
not even if you came out
of a prison, and begged me.

THE END OF THE AFFAIR

STEVE ORLEN

They set down their drinks, hug, kiss
For the final time, refuse, as they always have,
To say goodbye, and leave the hotel's bar
By different doors. Each hails a cab, drives
On different streets with similar views, city
Hustle-bustle anonymous, moving further
From the locus of their loss. Both cab radios
Play accompaniment, as though perfectly arranged:
The humdrum business of the business of the world,
Go here, go there, interrupted by that static
From the other dimension. Then the radio
Clarifies itself. It's definitely her voice. "Hey, you.
It's me. I didn't want to say goodbye. Now I want to."
The cabbie pushes a button. "Your turn, fella."
How did you do that? "We bring lovers
To each other and away. We are blind to one
And deaf to the other, though sensitive enough
To accommodate both anticipation and sorrow,
Which pay our bills on both accounts."

PENIS ENVY
AI

𝒞𝒢

My wife deserved to be shot.
I served time in the Gulf,
and I am telling you
when I came home and found her packed up and gone,
it wasn't long until I hatched a plan.
I located the man behind it all,
staked out his apartment and his job.
Then one afternoon, I dressed up in camouflage,
loaded my AK-47
and went to Hot Dog Heaven.
I found them in the parking lot,
sharing kisses over lunch.
I came up from behind, but changed my mind
and walked right in front,
and aimed through the windshield,
before they had a chance to see who it was.
I shouted my name, hoping she would hear as she died,
then I went to the passenger side
and fired at his head. A red mass
exploded like a sunburst.
At first, I couldn't believe I'd done it,
then I put the gun down
and looked at my hands, which were steady.
I pulled open the door,
before I knew what I was doing.
I just had to see what he was hiding in his pants.
It was pathetic, a sad, shriveled thing
there between his legs
and not the foot-long
she had said made her scream with pleasure.
I did hear screams, but they were coming

from my mouth, not hers.
Noise, I thought, as I fired at her body again.
Of course, I'd turned the gun on myself.
What else could I do to erase it all?—
the 911 calls, the sirens in the distance,
but the ordinariness of murder overwhelmed me,
possessed me like a spirit
and I thought how easy it would be
to take two or three more people with me.
Instead, I decided to give myself up,
plus I was out of ammunition.
I guess it is my destiny,
to be a living example for other men,
who are only bluffing when they threaten violence.
Now once a week, I write a column on relationships
for the prison publication.
I base my advice on actual situations.
For example, Clarence Thomas.
He had a dick fixation, just as I did.
For me, it was a torment and my downfall
and nearly his.
Ultimately, the question is always
how far are you willing to go?
I think within his parameters,
Clarence went the distance.
As far as I'm concerned,
he's earned his place on the Supreme Court
and stands tall beside all the other men,
who haven't given in to a woman's scorn,
who are born again from the fire of their ridicule.
If you ask me, Anita Hill got off too easily.
I would have caught the bitch
some afternoon, while the cherry blossoms
were in bloom
and boom, solved all my problems.
Oops! I think I wobbled over the line

that separates fantasy from crime.
The counselors tell me all the time
I've got to get it straight
how the imagination sometimes
races on without us.
But I know Debby and Ed are off somewhere
eating wedding cake
and letting me take the fall for their betrayal.
Is it fair that on the other side of this wall
Clarence has it all
and I have nothing but a ball and chain?
That reminds me, I checked this Othello play
out of the library.
It's about a guy
who loses his reputation and his wife,
well, he kills her, but she made him.
I found some parallels to my own life and Clarence's.
Othello's black.
But the other subtler thing is how a man
must stand up to humiliation,
must retaliate, or lose himself,
who when he finds some pubic hair
in his can of Coke
must ask, regardless of the consequences,
who put it there?

AFTER MAYAKOVSKY

Denis Johnson

It's after one. You're probably alone.
All night the moon rings like a telephone
in an empty booth above our separateness.
Now is the hour one answers. I am home.
Hello, my heart, my God, my President,
my darling: I'm alarmed by the alarm
clock's iridescent face, hung like a charm
from darkness's fat ear. This accident
that was my life will have its witnesses:
now, while the world lies wholly motionless
and sorry in a crapulence of stars,
now is the hour one rises to address
the ages and history and the universe:
I swear you'll never see my face again.

POST-THALAMION

J. Allyn Rosser

I. *An Open Fire*

I would not trace your steps
from here to all the world
and back—but there are dusks
that fall without you
when the gaslight will not catch
and I can sense your eyes on others,
pick up the scent of smiles
they cast on you. I concentrate
on flame, make dinner glow.

Later, you tend the blue light
of the evening news
strobing our overheated den
and lean closer
as if quickened by disaster,
rapt in a fabulous safety:
leaking toxins, gagging streams
and all the unsafe elsewhere
you, by watching, make stay there—

like the first man on earth
watching darkness through an open fire
at the mouth of his cave.
What he cannot quite make out
won't hurt *us*,
though it pass near enough
to fling fantastic shadow,
ripple through alerted blood
and lick the thinning, blackened air,
this flimsy air before us.

II. *Kiss Me You Fool*

Down on all fours, the morning after
your demon has scratched
the eyes out of mine,

I grope on the rug
for lost pieces of things,
some of them yours.

Your roses on the coffee table
level with me, sick
of craning their necks

over baby's breath
and bad language. They stick
all their tongues out at once.

Clearly they can't keep
putting up with this,
having gone to such crooked

lengths to be only beautiful, only
to die with flying colors.
You walk in, unshaven, just

as I find two petals, still
red, shaped like hearts.
Almost like hearts.

The height of passion's a cinch
to reach. Then what? A breeze
too strong for ripened parts?

III. *What Was Clear*

After the old friends and the new friends
and all the other guests were gone,
we sat at the table for hours
pondering contour and color,
forcing parts to interlock
and then thinking
better of it, thinking
maybe the puzzle was not
one, but two in one box.

No picture there to clue us in.
Still, edges were quickly complete
with corners and the usual sky.
On one side, the red of a barn
you called schoolhouse,
on the other, my cypress—
your oak. We squinted
and pressed, irritable
and hopeless by turns.

There was a lagoon at last,
with something there floating,
surely swans. But you laughed:
ducks. A white rowboat
after all, with a gap inside,
and something gray and something red
(two pieces we would never find).
A rag and a bucket, you said.
But it was a child with a pail.

IV. *Separation: Summer Night*

> "So I unto my selfe alone shall sing,
> The woods shall to me answere and my Eccho
ring."

— SPENSER, *Epithalamion*

Tonight the lamplight holds me derelict
at my desk, mocks me in yellow colors,
and sends a wire to every errant insect
within acres. I will screen such callers,
dismiss the Muses, brace each door that hinges
inward. There, love. I'll visit upon our honor
no reflection, but commune with what cringes
and crawls: all the clambering damned with torn or
hardened antennae, who've come so far to press
their tiny souls against the screen, grasping
at my little light, poor mecca of redress
for poorest mortals. Look: flattened, gasping,
they bear their flagging wings intact, and fight
to keep that tiny sense of self upright.

GHOST

ALAN SHAPIRO

Ghost of the living body
given shape and texture
by what the body is
denied, spectrum of desire
colorful when impeded,
white when not—since
at the end your love for me
was mostly fantasy,
and since fantasy became
a way of keeping faith,
of being present, let
it be your fantasy
tonight that I am here
beside you speaking, that
these words are mine.

Here you are just as you were
a year ago, remember?
on your birthday, you
in the dark den, in your lap
a shot glass full of what
around that time you took
to calling your vitamin h,
your vitamin happy, the tv
on, the sound off, the screen
crosshatched with rubbery
bands of color that
would spasm into tit
or ass a moment then
be gone, so that you couldn't
tell if what you saw

was seen or just imagined.
How long had it been
since you had touched me?

I was too sick to care
by then, or to think much
about what it was like
between us before the cancer,
those times we couldn't get
enough of one another,
and how we afterward
would lie there side by side,
my back to you, you with
an arm curled under me,
the other over, your hands
moving (unable not
to) up and down from rib
to nipple, nipple to rib,
as if you thought my body
were your undeserved
good luck. But that was then.

Now I was bald, I had
one breast, it was your birthday,
and I'd forgotten, hadn't
bought you anything,
not even a cake, and when
I woke and found you there
in the dark, the tv flashing
like bad nerves in the shot
glass you were lifting slowly
to your lips, I suddenly
really for the first
time knew how hard it must
have been for you to look
at me and not flinch, not wish

the doctor had taken both
of my breasts, instead of leaving
one behind, one freakish
remnant of a normal woman.

I got on my knees, I kneeled
before you, but before
I could ask you to forgive me,
what could I do to make
it up to you? you took
my head in both hands, tilted
it sideways, gently, saying,
go down on me, honey,
come on, it's been so long,
make me happy, you
can do that for me, can't you?

You should have known
that I was done with that
by then, too far inside
my body's misery
for sex, for you, for
anything beyond
my wanting not to suffer.
But now it's gone, the body,
the misery's gone too,
like a jammed channel
that's suddenly unjammed,
the picture unobstructed,
so I can see how generous
you feel, as I go down on you,
how blind but generous,
the way one hand is resting
on my face, my cheek,
to guide it, coax it while
the other hand is reaching

through my nightgown's
collar, to cup the one
breast tenderly, gratefully,
as if another swayed
beside it, and as I make
you happy, as your eyes
close, and you say my name,
say it softly, sadly,
as if it were another
woman's name, as if
I were the woman you
were cheating on me with,
I can see at last just
what it is you think
you're doing: it's your birthday,
and in two months I'll be dead.
This is the last time I will
touch you in this way.
It is your birthday, you
are celebrating, you
are happy, handsome, and
your wife is beautiful.

JUST THAT EMPTY
Patricia Smith

First, I put on your eyes. Then everywhere there are jewels,
rings of strawberry-tinged gold to wink from her fingers,
jade for her throat, grinning rhinestone tigers to droop from her ears.
Gems stutter in the light, and right away I say *yes, yes,* I try them
on myself, brilliance on my dry skin, then realize I don't want her
to love you too much. Away then, with the tiny rebel diamond and
the amethyst pin ringed in Austrian crystal. I take off your eyes.
The jewelry dulls, becomes the stuff of aged matrons, price tags
yellow in tall glass cases beyond any key. In two hours, I will meet
you and we will scream and ache and try to love with knives
at our throats. But right now I close my eyes and conjure
the outline of your wife. I play in her cornsilk hair, resent her smile,
touch her ears with a shaking finger. I force myself down her forearms
and between each of her fingers, I ride her hips and heartbeat,
then slide down her legs and sit, exhausted, in her shoes.
This, along with what you've told me, is all I know of her,
the woman who has you. You, who have me.

It is your wife's birthday. I am so bitterly and madly in love with you
that I volunteer to buy her gift while you are busy teaching words
to hungry writers. My soul is just that empty.

I consider brass diving helmets, tinkling music boxes,
a boxy raw cotton sheath, babushkas nestled in babushkas,
wacky lawn ornaments, a simple ivory egg, a tiny mandolin
and a Raggedy Ann doll. I sniff wildly expensive chocolates,
think of her name painted on silk with strokes as pale as air.
A sterling silver pen, kissed with an inlay of turquoise,
brings tears to my eyes. So do a dozen roses, carved of
burnished cherry wood, drooping as if they were alive
on the verge of death. Then I go totally wild, thinking

just let her see how mad he's become. I ask a clerk the price
of a clock shaped like Elvis with tiny blue suede shoes
riding the hour and minute hands, then I actually stand
in line holding a beautiful print of a black woman
with braids hiding half of her face. Time is running out,
and this search dizzies me. I don't want her clutching
the gaily wrapped box, falling in love all over again.

The Russian box whispers at me as I am about to rush past
another store, knowing that cold things would not interest her.
I love the wisps of gold, the delicacy of the icy colors,
and the salesclerks who dazzle me with fairy tales marred
by brusque accents thick as soup. Enthralled, I spend your
money, proud of myself, buying for the woman who is
my other me. She will kiss you deeply when she opens this,
and only that almost stops me, makes me want to flee
back to Elvis and his constantly orbiting blue shoes.
The raven-haired ladies lovingly wrap the box,
coo at my wisdom and insight, ask nosy questions at the
sight of cash, throw in the storybook for free. I wonder why
this is what I have chosen to move from your hand to hers.
Back in the hotel, I kiss you, babble and gesture, open the box,
show off the gleaming red enamel inside, and not out loud I pray
it is the box I hope it is, that when she lifts off the top
and looks inside, it will be full of the demons that dazzled Pandora.

WHY I WILL NOT GET OUT OF BED
JAMES TATE

My muscles unravel
like spools of ribbon:
there is not a shadow

of pain. I will pose
like this for the rest
of the afternoon,

for the remainder
of all noons. The rain
is making a valley

of my dim features.
I am in Albania,
I am on the Rhine.

It is autumn,
I smell the rain,
I see children running

through columbine.
I am honey,
I am several winds.

My nerves dissolve,
my limbs wither—
I don't love you.

I don't love you.

III
The Aftermath

EX-BOYFRIENDS
KIM ADDONIZIO

They hang around, hitting on your friends
or else you never hear from them again.
They call when they're drunk, or finally get sober,

they're passing through town and want dinner,
they take your hand across the table, kiss you
when you come back from the bathroom.

They were your loves, your victims,
your good dogs or bad boys, and they're over
you now. One writes a book in which a woman

who sounds suspiciously like you
is the first to be sadistically dismembered
by a serial killer. They're getting married

and want you to be the first to know,
or they've been fired and need a loan,
their new girlfriend hates you,

they say they don't miss you but show up
in your dreams, calling to you from the shoeboxes
where they're buried in rows in your basement.

Some nights you find one floating into bed with you,
propped on an elbow, giving you a look
of fascination, a look that says *I can't believe*

I've found you. It's the same way
your current boyfriend gazed at you last night,
before he pulled the plug on the tiny white lights

above the bed, and moved against you in the dark
broken occasionally by the faint restless arcs
of headlights from the freeway's passing trucks,

the big rigs that travel and travel,
hauling their loads between cities, warehouses,
following the familiar routes of their loneliness.

DIVORCED FATHERS AND PIZZA CRUSTS
MARK HALLIDAY

The connection between divorced fathers and pizza crusts
is understandable. The divorced father does not cook
confidently. He wants his kid to enjoy dinner.
The entire weekend is supposed to be fun. Kids love
pizza. For some reason involving soft warmth and malleability

kids approve of melted cheese on pizza
years before they will tolerate cheese in other situations.
So the divorced father takes the kid and the kid's friend
out for pizza. The kids eat much faster than the dad.
Before the dad has finished his second slice,

the kids are playing a video game or being Ace Ventura
or blowing spitballs through straws, making this hail
that can't quite be cleaned up. There are four slices left
and the divorced father doesn't want them wasted,
there has been enough waste already; he sits there

in his windbreaker finishing the pizza. It's good
except the crust is actually not so great—
after the second slice the crust is basically a chore—
so you leave it. You move on to the next loaded slice.
Finally there you are amid rims of crust.

All this is understandable. There's no dark conspiracy.
Meanwhile the kids are having a pretty good time
which is the whole point. So the entire evening makes
clear sense. Now the divorced father gathers
the sauce-stained napkins for the trash and dumps them

and dumps the rims of crust which are not
corpses on a battlefield. Understandability
fills the pizza shop so thoroughly there's no room
for anything else. Now he's at the door summoning the kids
and they follow, of course they do, he's a dad.

LOVER RELEASE AGREEMENT

J. ALLYN ROSSER

Against his lip, whose service has been tendered
lavishly to me, I hold no lien.
Here's his heart, which finally has blundered
from my custody. Here's his spleen.
Hereafter let your hair and eyes and breasts
be venue for his daydreams and his nights.
Here are smart things I've said, and all the rest
you'll hear about. Here are all our fights.
Now, whereas I waive rights to his kiss,
the bed you've shared with him has rendered null
his privilege in mine. Know that, and this:
undying love was paid to me in full.
No matter how your pleasures with him shine,
you'll always be comparing them to mine.

THE CHAIR

Stephen Berg

When he told me about the breakup of his marriage, about his wife fucking
other men now, (that's what he believed), that he wanted to die because
she wouldn't take him back,

Then, a year later, about being caught in the parking lot minutes after
he squeezed the metal and wood office chair into the trunk of his Honda
Prelude,

About not understanding why he stole it, why, even after he knew security
guards were watching, he continued to fit the chair into his trunk,

When the chair became the main theme of his suicidal shame, his help-
lessness, his endless daily calls, I felt some clue to the secret of his cure
had been revealed, though I had no idea what it was.

He needed to be forgiven, redeemed, but for what, after all? Surely not
for something as common as divorce, surely not for stealing a cheap chair
from the addiction clinic he ran.

I try to see him in the parking lot, lugging the worthless object to his
car, setting it down, unlocking the trunk, wrestling it in until he saw he
couldn't close it, jumping into the car, and a guard appears and asks what
he's doing.

"All I wanted, really, was to sit down, to rest..." I hear him say, and it's
crazy, it makes no sense—chairs are everywhere. Why steal a rickety old
chair from your employer?

Poor friend, what could have soothed your infinite need? Last night, in
a dream, bearded, disheveled, drained, exactly as you were, you sat so
close your breath and hair smelled real, you were hoping for a word, and

I yelled, "Go away! You're dead."
The guard's hand thrust through the car window, grabbing your shoulder, the transfixed menacing glare of glass and painted metal through the windshield at that instant, wild with detail…

But you can't describe the event, its textures and traits, shapes, gestures, light. You can only sketch auras of mood. Jeff, I'd ask you, and you'd be silent. You thought your confusion meant you had no right to speak. You believed words betrayed you, even in your poems where you grieve for an unnamed woman, for your soul infected with the silent wish to die, with the necessary theft of the chair. You equated silence with truth. I'd sit with you, day after day, helpless in your silence.

Two years after your wife demands you leave, hours after you slave all weekend to start a Japanese garden behind your new house, your heart stops, then the monthlong coma before the tubes are pulled and you dissolve.

Sit in it, feel it under you, relax; stand next to it, place your hand on its backrest; kneel, rest your head on its seat. Cool green steel legs, rivets, laminated wood.

The chair is an afterimage, a thing smoldering in the air.

Your final silence hums on the air.

December. Gray sun. Bamboo seedlings, grass, sky. Squatting to a rock that weighs much more than you do, your face crammed against it, you stretch your arms and hands around it; for the hundredth time, try to lift it, lean, kneel, clutch it tighter, squash your cheek and chest against it, grunt, jam your fingers under it, half-stand, push, hold your breath. Your life is like the darkness inside the rock, inside your brain.

The chair is a blindness that will kill you.

A MAN ALONE

STEVE ORLEN

I hated breaking up and I hated
Being left, finding myself in an apartment
With an extra set of silverware and a ghost,
Impatient to be gone. Then to summon up
Who I was before the bed was full with woman.
To shift the street-mind from *getting to*
To *slowing down and window shop*. In the bar down the street,
To let my eyes simplify again, and make no judgments,
And breathe in the smoke that drifts
Through one body then another,
And find myself close enough
To whisper into a woman's just-washed hair
And inhale that ten thousand year old scent.
To memorize a phone number.
To learn to say goodnight at her door.
To keep my hands in my pockets, like a boy.
To open the heart, only a little at a time.

DUSK

AMY GERSTLER

Dear, I can't subsist on this diet
(really more of a fast—celery
seed and a soft word every other
month) any longer. Is that blood
on your pillowcase or another girl's
lipstick? I want you to know
I've felt such unalloyed joy
over the past several decades,
smelling your hair and petting
your sweat-beaded feet while
you were asleep. It was far sweeter
than I ever thought possible.
But my ancestors are welling up
in me now and keep nudging me
towards the door. Bells are rung,
harps are played: recessional music.
We both know the theater will close
in a few minutes. If you had been
more attentive or a better pretender
I could have run on fumes for a few
more years, sipping snow melt,
remaining quite high on it. Let
the record show I recited prayers
for your perpetual ascension
and good health as I laid this note
in its frozen envelope on your desk
and left, taking both dogs, the teal
parakeet and the black cat with me.
They got custody of our love.

ONE MELODY

Tom Dvorske

It's not the biscuits and gravy nor the plastic
menu of this diner that brings you to mind.
Though I remember you in the booth next
to me, coy looks that hid—not too well—
what you never wanted to admit to yourself.
It's not you in that booth but her face is yours.
I want to ask her if her life is still possible.

I'm not looking for revenge.
I don't care how you'd look at me now,
or if you even still think of me. I'm certain
of the answer and it brings no feeling. I call
her your name. She looks at me as at an accident.
I insist she's you. She assures me, *no*. I tell her
I would have left her anyway, better that she
moved out the weekend I was out of town
visiting my friend in the state hospital.

She grows hostile, asks for the check and tells
me to *fuck off*. That I don't understand a thing
about how she feels, or about what she's gone
through. Moreover, that I've got the details
all wrong. She didn't move out. I did. The U-haul
pulling away as she returned from her weekend
at the lake. I start to think I'm imagining this.
She reminds me that it was *I* who contrived
our cohabitation. It was *I* who assumed
that through my gratuitous gestures of love
she would see that I was meant for her. She
says things don't work this way, and that I
may as well forget about it because if I don't
want anything, then why am I even asking?
I tell her I thought she was someone else.

AFTER

MARTHA RHODES

After the *Now it's over,*
even the cutting boards split.
The recliner locks upright,
the ottoman refuses her legs,
the bathroom her spillage.
There is a chair, a rope, a beam.

But for the one who sits at his desk
humming, the day is gloriously lit.
How to stretch that light to her corner?
Or leave her corner? Or sing—
if only to show him she can, despite—
when her voice is a cracked tweet.

A friend urges, *Imagine a pitiless*
and without dark place. But for her,
the swim up river is easy. Familiar
the blind passage back to that moment
before, before he, who waited hungry
on that river's bank, pulled her out,

if not to devour her in the breathless open,
then to do what, and for how long,
and then, what after?

WHAT TO WEAR FOR DIVORCE
Angela Ball

Bats in your hair,
But only if they can hang upside down
Properly.

Putty on your hands,
Butter in your mouth.

Be the feather in someone's cap,
The spyglass in the pirate's hand,
The podiatrist's foot, asleep.

Be the bewildered woman
Half lifting her skirts to cross a muddy street
While a rain cloud watches.

Wear something worn first
By a wolf.

GREEN COUCH
EDWARD HIRSCH

That was the year I lived without fiction
and slept surrounded by books on the unconscious.
I woke every morning to a sturdy brown oak.

That was the year I left behind my marriage
of twenty-eight years, my faded philosophy books, and
the green couch I had inherited from my grandmother.

After she died, I drove it across the country
and carried it up three flights of crooked stairs
to a tiny apartment in West Philadelphia,

and stored it in my in-laws basement in Bethesda,
and left it to molder in our garage in Detroit
(my friend Dennis rescued it for his living room),

and moved it to a second-floor study in Houston
and a fifth-floor apartment on the Upper West Side
where it will now be carted away to the dump.

All my difficult reading took place on that couch
which was turning back into the color of nature
while I grappled with ethics and the law,

the reasons for Reason, Being and Nothingness,
existential dread and the death of God
(I'm still angry at Him for no longer existing).

That was the year that I finally mourned
for my two dead fathers, my sole marriage,
and the electric green couch of my past.

Darlings, I remember everything.
But now I try to speak the language of
the unconscious and study earth for secrets.

I go back and forth to work.
I walk in the botanical gardens on weekends
and take a narrow green path to the clearing.

BEGINNING WITH HIS BODY AND ENDING IN A SMALL TOWN

KIM ADDONIZIO

It's true I can't forget any part of him,
not the long vein rising up along the underside of his cock,
or the brushy hair around his balls, dank star of the asshole,
high arches of his feet, strawberry mole on his left cheek—
imperfection that made his face exquisite—
and the freckles scattered over his back,
white insides of his wrists, I remember those too,
and the scar on his belly oh I'm kissing it now,
he belongs to me so purely now he's left me,
he'll never come back, his face as he lets go inside me,
I'll never see it again, I stand dripping
in the shower where I once knelt
before him to drink whatever came
out of him, sometimes he would watch
me as I walked naked around the room,
here I am, it's the same room, I'm still
seeing his face the night it closed
to me forever like a failed business, iron grillwork
across the door, dirty windows, trash scattered
over the floor and the fixtures taken out, I turned
away and stumbled down the street, the one bar
was open, the saddest bar in the world, filled
with painted clowns and a few drunks, the owner had passed out
in a booth, covered by his coat, his girlfriend was working
and said *The usual, right?* and I couldn't say a word
except *Please*, and I took a stool and drank
what she served and served and served.

TALKING RICHARD WILSON BLUES, BY RICHARD CLAY WILSON

Denis Johnson

You might as well take a razor
to your pecker as let a woman in your heart.
First they do the wash and then they kill you.
They flash their lights and teach your wallet to puke.
They bring it to you folded—if you see her
stepping between the coin laundry and your building
over the slushy street and watch the clothing steam,
you can't wait to open up the door when she puts
the stairs behind her and catch that warmth between you.
It changes into a baby. "Here's to the little shitter,
the little linoleum lizard." Once he peed on me
when I was changing him—that one got a laugh
from the characters I wasted all my chances with
at Popeye's establishment when it was over
by the Wonderland. But it's destroyed
now and I understand one of those shopping malls
that are like great monuments of blindness
and folly stands there. And next door,
the grimy restaurants of men with movies
where they used to wear human faces,
the sad people from space. But that was never me,
because everything in those days depended on my work.
"Listen, I'm going to work," was all I could say,
and drunk or sober I would put on the uniform
of Texaco and wade into my life.
I felt like a man of honor of substance,
but the situation was dancing underneath me—
once I walked into the living room at my sister's
and saw that the two of them, her and my sister,
had turned sometime behind my back not exactly

fatter, but heavy, or squalid, with cartoons
moving across the television in front of them,
surrounded by laundry, and a couple of Coca-Colas
standing up next to the iron on the board.
I stepped out into the yard of bricks
and trash and watched the light light
up the blood inside each leaf,
and I asked myself, Now what is the rpm
on this mother? Where do you turn it on?
I think you understand how I felt.
I'm not saying everything changed in the space
of one second of seeing two women, but I did
start dragging her into the clubs with me. I insisted
she be sexy. I just wanted to live.
And I did: some nights were so
sensory I felt the starlight landing on my back
and I believed I could set fire to things with my fingers—
but the strategies of others broke my promise.
At closing time once, she kept talking to a man
when I was trying to catch her attention to leave.
It was a Negro man, and I thought of black limousines
and black masses and black hydrants filled
with black water. When the lights came on
you could see all kinds of intentions in the air.
I thought I might smack her face, or spill a glass,
but instead I opened him up with my red fishing knife
and took out his guts and I said, "Here they are,
motherfucker, nigger, here they are."
There were people frozen around us. The lights had just come on.
At that moment I saw her reading me and reading me
from the end of the world where I saw her standing,
and the way the sacred light played across her face
all I can tell you is I had to be a diamond
of ice to manage. Right down the middle from beginning to end
my life pours into one ocean: into this prison
with its empty ballfield and its empty

preparations for Never Happen.
If she ever comes to visit me, to hell with her,
I won't talk to her, and my son can entertain
himself. God kill them both. I'm sorry for nothing.
I'm just an alien from another planet.
I am not happy. Disappointment
lights its stupid fire in my heart,
but two days a week I staff
the Max Security laundry above the world
on the seventh level, looking at two long roads
out there that go to a couple towns.
Young girls accelerating through the intersection
make me want to live forever,
they make me think of the grand things,
of wars and extremely white, quiet light that never dies.
Sometimes I stand against the window for hours
tuned to every station at once, so loaded on crystal
meth I believe I'll drift out of my body.
Jesus Christ, your doors close and open,
you touch the maniac drifters, the fire-eaters,
I could say a million things about you
and never get that silence out of time
that happens when the blank muscle hangs
between its beats—that is what I mean
by darkness, the place where I kiss your mouth,
where nothing bad has happened.
I'm not anyone but I wish I could be told
when you will come to save us. I have written
several poems and several hymns, and one
has been performed on the religious
ultrahigh frequency station. And it goes like this.

LONGING
DONNA MASINI

Once we were together
I missed just sitting beside him, in a crowded
room, say, his sleeve rolled
just below the elbow, the muscle
swelling. It was promise, it was Catherine and
Heathcliff, the phone call that might
come. Then it was just another part of him.
Just an arm. But just
now I thought of him, I thought yes, the arm.
His arm. His *arm*.
Now that it's over it is luminous again.

DIVORCE
KEVIN PRUFER

All of the names have been changed
Someone had entered the yard that night

In order to protect the innocent,
My mother, we'll call her Cynthia,

Was in the kitchen watering the plants
That decorated the country house windows

When suddenly she heard a sawing from the woods,
This is a true story,

Out back behind the house
When a strange man

Cut the largest tree with a crash into the moss
And such a cloud of dust and birds

Rose to the treetops and beyond

*

Mine was the wisp of hair that came lovingly to her cheek
Mine was the breath against the silk of the blouse

But whose was the saw that leveled the tree,
And the second tree? One by one,

The trees fell, and this, a true story,
Though the names have been changed,

The two of us afraid, in a way,
In the dark, even to open

The front door and call into the black woods,
Though I, only a child, we'll call me

By my own name,
And she, Cynthia, tangled in all this

Watering can in hand, paused
Over the spider plant and the dishes not even done,

The Jeep parked on the gravel drive,
Not a telephone between there and town,

And my father—we'll call him that—
Who knew what he was thinking

At that very moment What could we do? So
To protect the innocent

We turned off the house lights one by one
Locked the doors as, at that very moment,

A laughing from the woods just outside the house

★

Difficult to describe, though it sounded not unlike
The sound of the saw if I must make it clear

Up, up into the attic we crawled
And out with those lights, too, until

In retrospect, in the darkness,
There were so many things that horrible year:

The bursting of dams, my brother also gone, the letters
Always laughing in the mailbox, and forever somewhere

Someone, anonymous, hungry
Mine was the crying into Cynthia's skirt,

Mine was, finally, the lost-in-sleep
In the air beneath the attic window,

With the nameless man in the yard,
That, by sunup, was scattered with the black half-fingers

Of this, the strange true story, the remains of our trees.

THE MONARCHS: 47
ALISON HAWTHORNE DEMING

What he never understood
was that his lying
drove me crazier than
his infidelity. He was obvious
with his flirtations,
sloppy with his lies,
flaunting the evidence
as if he wanted me
to police him toward what
he thought he wanted to be—
a good man, a good partner,
kind and loyal. That
fantasy I too believed,
because of a certain tenderness
that opened between us
during his telling how,
when his father lay dying,
he had come to the bedside,
the nurse coaching him
as the patient's breathing
changed—"Now. Take his hands"—
and he had done so, learning
in that moment (he said this
with a sincerity that never
returned once we started
living together) more about
life than about death,
about being responsible.
A year after he left me,
he sent his forwarding address
in a self-flagellating letter—

no details except the transition
had gone harder than planned.
I already knew through friends
of his latest fling—the woman
he'd left town with, already
history. Warn her, I joked
to a mutual friend, thinking
of the new one in my place,
in her place, in hers and hers.

EXCAVATING THE RUINS OF MIAMI BEACH
GERALD COSTANZO

After months of drilling
and digging, of carving out
the central trench,

they had come down
through layers of soil and cement,
through sand rife with shells—

ample debris of a Cenozoic sea-bed—
to arrive at the entrance
of a narrow hollow. A phalanx

entering the darkness,
they were astonished, as they lowered
themselves beneath the rotted

ceiling timbers, at the reflections
their lights gave back
of objects fastened to the walls.

Ancient pictographs—
all the artifacts one could covet
in a findspot. The names

had been affixed
in an archaic plastic script,
decipherable in shallow

embossing: Big Daddy and Dr. Erwin
Stillman; Big Daddy and Patty Duke.
This in the midst of something

called a Hot Dog Stand
in the fallen United States. Big
Daddy and Shecky Greene.

Here was the patriarch
in a thousand proofs, his Little
Mama with her buxom personality.

They began to dust and wash
the relics of this fossil beach,
to preserve something

of their own history. Big Daddy
and Norm Crosby. Big Daddy
and Totie Fields and Jerry Vale.

And since this *was all* they knew—
all this much—
they assumed they knew it all.

APPROACH

Amy Gerstler

How could I lose sight of him? I only know that my eyes followed him as far as possible, till my gaze wandered over the horizon's brink, where insight and blindness alike are insufficient. When I go for a walk in the afternoon to mail letters, avoiding my own eyes in windows or water, I frequently have the feeling I'm just about to see him. When I get into bed at night, all bundled up, the bedclothes exhale a whiff reminiscent of him, though he's never set foot in this room. Tonight I click off the light and lie on my back, my hands behind my head as though I were lying in wet grass, waiting for rabbits and deer to leap over me, or something heavier to puncture my stomach with its hoof. I wait for my eyes to adjust to the darkness, then for the night birds to begin sounding off. I think about him for what seems like a long time, and about how sad it is that what I jot down daily, or mull over in the walled chamber behind my eyes, can't hold a candle to his flickering image, can't show me some fresh vision of him, or explain why I constantly feel, as I drift off, that he's watching me.

HEAVY TRASH
MARK HALLIDAY

What is that man doing?
He is clumping through the snow toward the municipal trash barrel
next to General Wayne Park.

What is in the black trash bag he is carrying?
It looks so heavy!
It is amazingly heavy. It contains
two Philadelphia phonebooks and a Children's Health Encyclopedia
and three drawing pads and an illustrated history of baseball.

That's all? That doesn't sound so heavy.
But they are full of ice—that is, they have become
blocks of pulp stiff with frozen rain.

Explain.
I will explain, I want to explain.
He is a divorced father.   *Sherlock*

And?
And divorced fathers cannot evade absurdities.

Is that an explanation?
There was an apartment... Then the trunk of an old car...

What is he doing now?
He is pounding the trash bag with a stone from a stone wall
to make it fit down into the trash barrel.

Should he be arrested?
No. The police have less absurd things to focus on.

Is there meaning in this?
It's about how some endings never end.

EQUITABLE DISTRIBUTION

J. ALLYN ROSSER

In the mall of ever after and true love
We separate and shop around, aghast,
For things we never thought of getting two of.

Dodging jewelers we'd once played the fool of,
Prowling racks past season, thinking fast
In the mall of ever after and true love,

We browse through needs the other never knew of,
Inspect, and drastically discount, the past
We never once thought we'd make two of.

Let's each trade rings for one more turtle dove
And break whatever bonds cannot be cashed
In the mall of ever after and true love.

I'll keep the house and child in lieu of you, love.
You keep the car and all the photographs
We never did think to take two of.

Before our overheated hearts cool off,
We'll beat them back in shape to be recast
In the mall of ever after for more true love,
One thing we never thought we would need two of.

A MAY-DECEMBER ROMANCE

RAVI SHANKAR

Wide, woven, the brim of a straw hat shades
Her eyes as she leans against a stack of crates,
The dock buzzing with arrival and departure.

She holds in one hand a bouquet of nosegays,
Straightens the other arm as if to feed a gull.
The speck of his ship has long since vanished

And now sunlight glances off a barge's prow,
Reveals again a shopworn tale. Deeply, she inhales.
Everything is predestined in retrospect.

A fisherman lugs a tub of ice onto a lanyard deck.
The wind stirs an abandoned hank of rope,
Lifts her linen dress until it reveals red kneecaps.

What was the last thing he murmured to her?
She remembers nothing save the way
His chin, unshaven, felt against her tongue.

A clomp of boots breaks her uneven respiration.
Momentarily, she'll fling the bouquet into seas
The color of gray she has never before seen.

STRAIGHT BOYFRIEND
PETER COVINO

I have had to let you go—
red balloon, skyscraper

like a bustling city, a cigarette break,
a charging ram.

Not without a little sadness,
flowering pear trees of East 22nd Street,

canopy, bouquet, petals-ful of mess,
pure, unadulterated

the way you take up the oxygen
and bounteous colors

all of two weeks. I have avoided
the gym, the fleece jacket

and especially the Elvis LPs.
The thought of you—

a thousand slipknots,
gait and pubic hair

squint and twitter,
revved engine, last sip,

puff of smoke.

ANNULMENT
ANGELA BALL

I've ruined my marriage, but still I enjoy the hum of nature,
And the pleasure of greeting a kindly pedestrian
When I have the chance.

Make no mistake, I'm fond of my bungalow.
Returning home at night, I can't resist waltzing a bit
With my valise. I let my right foot go first,
Since it's my favorite.

I live a quiet life, thinking of what to say,
Heeding the call of the wild, removing my sunglasses in tunnels.
I never refreeze, though I may try it one day.

THE GIFT
David Lehman

> "He gave her class. She gave him sex."
> —Katherine Hepburn
> on Fred Astaire and Ginger Rogers

℘

He gave her money. She gave him head.
He gave her tips on "aggressive growth" mutual funds. She gave him a red
    rose and a little statue of Eros.
He gave her Genesis 2 (21-23). She gave him Genesis 1 (26-28).
He gave her a square peg. She gave him a round hole.
He gave her Long Beach on a late Sunday in September. She gave him zin-
nias
    and cosmos in the plenitude of July.
He gave her a camisole and a brooch. She gave him a cover and a break.
He gave her Venice, Florida. She gave him Rome, New York.
He gave her a false sense of security. She gave him a true sense of uncer-
tainty.
He gave her the finger. She gave him what for.
He gave her a black eye. She gave him a divorce.
He gave her a steak for her black eye. She gave him his money back.
He gave her what she had never had before. She gave him what he had
had
    and lost.
He gave her nastiness in children. She gave him prudery in adults.
He gave her Panic Hill. She gave him Mirror Lake.
He gave her an anthology of drum solos. She gave him the rattle of leaves
    in the wind.

ALL THE WAY FROM THERE TO HERE

JACK GILBERT

From my hill I look down on the freeway and over
to a gull lifting black against the grey ridge.
It lifts slowly higher and enters the bright sky.
Surely our long, steady dying brings us to a state
of grace. What else can I call this bafflement?

From here I deal with my irrelevance to love.
With the bewildering tenderness of which I am
composed. The sun goes down and comes up again.
The moon comes up and goes down. I live
with the morning air and the different airs of night.
I begin to grow old.

The ships put out and are lost.
Put out and are lost.
Leaving me with their haunting awkwardness
and the imperfection of birds. While all the time
I work to understand this happiness I have come into.

What I remember of my nine-story fall
down through the great fir is the rush of green.
And the softness of my regret in the ambulance going
to my nearby death, looking out at the trees leaving me.

What I remember of my crushed spine
is seeing Linda faint again and again,
sliding down the white X-ray room wall
as my sweet body flailed on the steel table
unable to manage the bulk of pain. That
and waiting in the years after for the burning
in my fingertips, which would announce,
the doctors said, the beginning of paralysis.

What I remember best of the four years of watching
in Greece and Denmark and London and Greece is Linda
making lunch. Her blondeness and ivory coming up
out of the blue Aegean. Linda walking with me daily
across the island from Monolithos to Thíra and back.
That's what I remember most of death:
the gentleness of us in that bare Greek Eden,
the beauty as the marriage steadily failed.

LESSENING

Linda Gregg

Without even looking in the album
I realized suddenly, two months later,
you had stolen the picture of me.
The one in color in the Greek waves.
After you had hurt me so much,
how could you also take the picture
from me of a time before I knew you?
When I was with Jack.
Steal the small proof that once
I lived well, was loved
and beautiful.

SPIDER PLANT
MICHAEL RYAN

When I opened my eyes this morning,
the fact of its shooting out
long thin green runners on which miniatures
of the mother will sprout,
and that each of these offshoots
could in its own time repeat this,
terrified me. And something seemed awful
in the syllables of the word "Brenda,"
sounding inside me before they made a name,
then making a name of no one I've known.
I had been dreaming I was married to Patty
again. She kept coming on my tongue
and I knew if I put myself in
we'd have to stay together this time.
But I wanted to, and did, and as I did
the sadness and pleasure of our nine years together
washed through me as a river, yet
I knew this wasn't right, it couldn't
work, and though we were now enmeshed
forever, I began to rise from my body
making love with her on the bed and to hover
at a little distance over both of us.
That's when I awoke and saw the spider plant.

X

THE MONARCHS: 43
ALISON HAWTHORNE DEMING

Butterflies rise in courtship, but
people fall in love. I'm thinking
what fun a talk-show host would make of
my romantic accidents and failures,
the heeding of blessed appetite
when it teases, *This is how to survive, girl* !
even when you know it's a wrong thing to desire.

                      I'm thinking
about my friend, our lunches
sprinkled over the past two years
in which, after we covered the business
of our books and agents, we turned
to the tiresome topic
of our loneliness, how we know
what we won't give up
for love—not wanting to fall
from what we've built alone and wondering
if this makes us incapable of
having what we want.
                      I'm thinking
of another friend, long married,
after hearing of the in-house
separation—that trial,
that desperation—when one partner begins
to rupture out of his former self
not knowing what he's becoming
only that without breaking
what he was
he will be broken.

                    I'm thinking
of a woman who embraces her marriage
by juggling lovers on the side—
"impure," she calls herself,
try "European," I advise. This
strategy came to her only after
her husband's affair, and she promised
her wounded self to draw a border
he would never cross.

HALF-LIFE
Bob Hicok

The question was, which of your old lovers
would you most like to meet in a bar fight?
I thought of you smashing a beer bottle
on the edge of a table into a violent bloom
of glass. Since chaos is some cousin
to how we made love, you were wearing nothing
but a slip and I was heartfelt in my nakedness.
By now you can tell none of this is true,
as I can tell you're not really here, talking with me,
as you have not been here talking with me
for twenty-five years. See the mistake
in that sentence that isn't a mistake, how bodies
ghost, voices vine through the dendrites,
how even withdrawn, a touch that was once love
persists as touch. Weaker, yes, by the hour,
and new fingerprints intercede,
and when I paint the ceiling today
you'll not be with me on the ladder,
and the forty kisses I share with my wife
won't even implicate your lips. But every time
half of you disappears, half remains, a Greek
said something about this, that the severed weed
leaves a root, to always put the top
back on the peanut butter. And though I'm not sure
what size shoe you wore or color you adored,
I feel you had a pulse, that you knew how to walk,
I sense there was a period when our lives
overlapped, when we found ourselves
in the same rooms, the same bed, inserting, holding,
licking, doing all the maintenance
couples do to pretend that skin

doesn't end where skin ends but is the beginning
of planets and music, of everything, that's all we want,
everything. It's good to imagine you out there,
not thinking of but sensing me as a shadow
might feel the air through which it glides,
good to put down my fists, to no longer fight
that I will always be pregnant with you.

CHARADES

Edward Hirsch

We waited on two sides of the subway tracks.
You were riding uptown and I was heading downtown
to a different apartment, after all these years.

We were almost paralyzed, like characters
in a Beckett play, and then you started
to pantomime, as in charades.

First, you touched your right eye
and then your left knee
and then you pointed toward me.

I made a sign of understanding
and then the train suddenly roared
into the station, and you disappeared.

MORE OR LESS A SORROW

Jane Miller

What do I see? The lightless past.
It's talk. It kept us going
between lovemaking. And while I was not you
I discovered how truly fascinating you were,
bleaching your hair and removing your underwear
for me as much as for you, gestures I took
seriously all the way back to their beginnings
in parody and on TV. But
after we went all that way I found a heart
on a stick, hopping among the fresh desert
sage, and even then it was great
to be alone. Somewhere between the middle
and the end of our long talk we ended
up inside, touched but never seen
which we must have had trouble believing in,
tender as it was, otherworldly, like an idea
finally devoid of meaning, the pure feeling
of coming outdoors, finding no one watching,
nothing moving in the steady wind.
The rest of the time I felt was always
a premonition of my first night alone,
the phantom hotel of my forties,
this helpless country. If ever I was ready
to live a life, by evening
what have I done? I hurt you, all over
nothing, a trifle, as things go. Noise
on the brain, habitually tooled
to the point it drove us practically
insane, and we had to notice, I suppose,
that inside this world
is another more—it must have to do

with our placement—full of people
with questions rather than choices.
There I found you experience
through your heart and soul—very noble—
while I experience through my nights and days,
a vague union—maybe it'll save me,
maybe it's a waste—

SWAY

DENIS JOHNSON

Since I find you will no longer love,
from bar to bar in terror I shall move
past Forty-third and Halsted, Twenty-fourth
and Roosevelt where fire-gutted cars,
their bones the bones of coyote and hyena,
suffer the light from the wrestling arena
to fall all over them. And what they say
blends in the tarantellasmic sway
of all of us between the two of these:
harmony and divergence,
their sad story of harmony and divergence,
the story that begins
I did not know who she was
and ends *I did not know who she was.*

THE MONARCHS: 20

ALISON HAWTHORNE DEMING

I remember a line from some classic
movie—that nature gives us loneliness
so we'll find each other. Coming out
of bad love—a man with a bag of tricks
and evasions that he flaunted from the start
and couldn't stop, even when he wanted to,
which I believe he genuinely did want
to do, though some emotional template
stopped him—I know there's no more room in me
for that kind of hurt. The moral sense,
I told a friend after the relationship was over,
is like the back or the knee, a rough draft,
long way to go before it works as well
as the tongue, the cock, or the stomach.
My good friend listened, while we drove
the old La Honda Road, keying wildflowers
in his field guide, then stopping on the coast
to savor oysters at Duarte's, then check out
tidepools, brack and lunge of wave slosh,
where a single anemone, like a feathery uterus,
waved its lacy gullet in the tidal breeze.
Only one, I thought, how strange, until
together we found the others, dozens
stranded above the tide, their bodies
closed like fists, camouflaged to match
the rocks on which they'd grown.

LOOKING DOWN THE BARREL

Tom Dvorske

It's 5 a.m. and this candle is burned down
to a nub like my drug-limp penis.

A car narrates the intersection.
Stop lights blink, de-programmed

for another hour at least. It's cold
though my open window admits no

wind, only raucous bird songs that
hemorrhage in my eyes.

I'm practicing to forget, so when
I've forgotten it will surely never return.

This requires discipline, active
reenactment of what must be forgotten

so that forgetting affirms the absence
of purpose, ritual.

I'm constructing a culture.
The will to exclude is the first rule.

The second: to exclude.
The third: worse. And

the fourth: extreme prejudice.
One must be tolerant of these ideas

to affect larger issues.
There is no other way;

the object of exclusion does not matter.
Go ahead. Pick anything.

GOODBYE

PATRICIA SMITH

dear you this is just the thousandth time
I have written these words there are slivers
of my bone in them there are whole oceans
of cry I have written these words to only me and
used them to sing myself to sleep I have
chanted them to recover from your smell
on my body but tonight they are your words
you own them because tonight I looked in
your eyes and could not find myself in them
because you held my shoulders and told
me to be patient again not to give up on you
not to give up on us and I am tired of being
the strong one, tired of hanging on, swinging
from that one thin hook of your heart,
I want to sleep now I want to sleep now I
want to scrub you away forget your face
I want not to hate myself anymore not to nod
yes yes again like a dog craving shelter not to
smile indulgent when you call me her or use
the circle of my arms to cry for her I want
to sleep I want to sleep sleep now in arms that
aren't so crowded this brand of love this yes
but no not really love has wearied me I
want to be whole with someone I want a whole
someone I want to hold someone and you
tell me you will not be much of a man and I
say yes and you tell me you may hurt forever
and I say yes and you say this is hard for me
and have you noticed the hundred places my heart
is buried under the floorboard on the highway
in the telephone wire in every syllable of every

pulling back pulling away that is you yes these
are your words now these are your words for
free I cannot wear them anymore I cannot dress
myself in them or feed on them it is not enough
to know I can say goodbye not enough anymore
for you to tell me how strong I am pat on
the back not enough the please don't worry kiss
not enough your craving closure not enough
not even the crazy eyes and sweat you are now
is enough I was not in your eyes tonight I want
to sleep just sleep just wake up in a world where
I am not waiting and you are not loving me to death
goodbye
goodbye
end this: love, patricia
end this love. Patricia.

BLUE VASE

ALAN SHAPIRO

Now and again, I look up as I clean,
and the large room we quarreled over,
arranging and rearranging it all week,
surprises me this morning, stiller somehow
for the tangled shadowy commotion light
is making on the freshly painted walls
and varnished floors, around you working there
bent over at the table. Slowly you run
the hem of what will be our bedroom curtains
under the needle pumping faster now,
now slower, blurring and coming into view.
I think my things begin to seem less shy
here next to yours: our couches at an angle,
quilted with shadows which the sunlight weaves
and unweaves all day long, day after day;
your oak chest in between them, and on the chest
a lamp and small blue vase my ex-wife left
behind so many months ago. Blue vase,
and lamp, and couch, the table where you sew—
suddenly for the first time they remind me
not so insistently of my old place,
the other rooms in which I once arranged them
as carefully as we have now, as though for good.
Suddenly for the first time I can imagine
being years from my last thought of her,
that past life, old intimacies, the small talk—
tender or quarrelsome—our days and nights
unfolded in those rooms only, nowhere else.

Even if months from now some small detail
should come to mind, hearing myself say something

she would say, her voice entangled with
my voice a moment, I know now it will come
only to prove how easily I had
forgotten it till then, how easily
it is relinquished. I dust the blue vase off.
I buff it to a stringent sheen.
How odd that I should have to tell myself,
today, I was at home there all those years,
woven into that intricate design
so deeply, sadly, certain it was durable
if only because it seemed to fray so long.
And though a long time after I would struggle
to believe it was my leaving, not living there,
that made those rooms seem magical, today
it's the belief itself that saddens me:
it comes so easily. What saddens me today
is that I'm home.
                              You call me over.
You're smiling because the curtains in your hands—
white curtains with blue flowers and yellow flowers—
fall everywhere about you, fold on fold,
as you try to hold them up. And I smile too,
taking the other edge, surprised how much
I have to lean back, one knee bent, to keep
that plentiful bright cloth above the floor
it grazes now, no matter what I do.

PART OF ME WANTING EVERYTHING TO LIVE

Linda Gregg

This New England kind of love reminds me
of the potted chrysanthemum my husband
gave me. I cared for it faithfully,
turning the pot a quarter turn each day
as it sat by the window. Until the blossoms
hung with broken necks on the dry stems.
Cut off the dead parts and watched
green leaves begin, new buds open.
Thinking the chrysanthemum would not die
unless I forced it to. The new flowers
were smaller and smaller, resembling
little eyes awake and alone in the dark.
I was offended by the lessening,
by the heap renewal. By a going on
that gradually left the important behind.
But now it's different. I want the large
and near, and endings more final. If it must
be winter, let it be absolutely winter.

AT THE END OF THE AFFAIR
MAXINE KUMIN

That it should end in an Albert Pick hotel
with the air conditioner gasping like a carp
and the bathroom tap plucking its one-string harp
and the sourmash bond half gone in the open bottle,

that it should end in this stubborn disarray
of stockings and car keys and suitcases,
all the unfoldings that came forth yesterday
now crammed back to overflow their spaces,

considering the hairsbreadth accident of touch
the nightcap leads to—how it protracts
the burst of colors, the sweetgrass of two tongues,
then turns the lock in Hilton or in Sheraton,
in Marriott or Holiday Inn for such
a man and woman—bearing in mind these facts,

better to break glass, sop with towels, tear
snapshots up, pour whiskey down the drain
than reach and tangle in the same old snare
saying the little lies again.

LANDSCAPE WITH A WOMAN
RICHARD SHELTON

when shadows climb
out of the desert
up the sides of mountains
and violent birds pass like projectiles
on their way home for the night
I say I have given you
everything it was all I had

when darkness rises
to the tops of the saguaros
and a river of cool air begins to flow
down the arroyo
I say I have given you
little it was all I had

when the moon
sits on top of the Santa Ritas
then levitates becoming smaller
and more pale as it goes
I say I have given you
nothing it was all I had

but you do not listen you go on
into your losses without birds
without mountains or shadows
or the moon you look into yourself
and say it is not enough
it was never enough

Permissions

Acknowledgments

Many thanks go to the following individuals and institutions without whose assistance and unfaltering support this project would not otherwise have been possible: Elizabeth Clementson, Gerald Costanzo, Jhari Derr-Hill, Mark Halliday, Kira Henehan, Bob Hicok, Edward Hirsch, Emily Hyland, Cynthia Lamb, Marymount Manhattan College, Peter Naccarato, Yaronit Nordin, Steve Orlen, Poets House, Kevin Prufer, Michael Romanos, Shelby Stokes, and Carlin Wragg.

About the Contributors

KIM ADDONIZIO's latest books are *Lucifer at the Starlite* and *Ordinary Genius: A Guide for the Poet Within*. She has also authored two novels, *Little Beauties* and *My Dreams Out in the Street*. Her awards include two National Endowment for the Arts Fellowships and a Guggenheim. She teaches privately in Oakland, California, and online at www.kimaddonizio.com.

AI is the author of seven books, including *Vice*, which won the National Book Award in 1999. She is a Professor of English at Oklahoma State University.

ANGELA BALL's books of poetry include *Kneeling Between Parked Cars*, *Possession*, *Quartet*, and *The Museum of the Revolution*. Her newest collection, *Night Clerk at the Hotel of Both Worlds*, published by the University of Pittsburgh Press in 2007, received both the Mississippi Institute of Arts and Letters Award and the Donald Hall Prize from the Association of Writers and Writing Programs. The recipient of a Fellowship from the National Endowment for the Arts, she is a Professor of English at the Center for Writers at the University of Southern Mississippi.

STEPHEN BERG's most recent books are *Cuckoo's Blood*; *The Elegy on Hats*; and *Rimbaud: Versions & Intentions (...still unilluminated I...)*.

GERALD COSTANZO teaches in the Creative Writing Program at Carnegie Mellon University and serves as Director of Carnegie Mellon University Press. His most recent collections of poems are *Great Disguise* and *Nobody Lives on Arthur Godfrey Boulevard*. He has received two National Endowment for the Arts Fellowships as well as Fellowships from the Pennsylvania Council on the Arts and the Falk Foundation. He lives in Mt. Lebanon, Pennsylvania, and in Portland, Oregon.

PETER COVINO is an Assistant Professor of English and Creative Writing at the University of Rhode Island. Winner of the 2007 PEN America/Osterweil Award for Emerging Poets, he is the author of *Cut Off the Ears of Winter* as well as the chapbook *Straight Boyfriend*. Recent poems have appeared in *The Paris Review*, *Colorado Review*, *Gulf Coast*, and others. He is also the founding editor of *Barrow Street*.

ALISON HAWTHORNE DEMING's most recent book of poems is *Rope* (Penguin, 2009). She teaches at the University of Arizona and lives in Tucson. She is currently completing a nonfiction book with the working title *Murder, Raft, & Exaltation: A Bestiary for the 21st Century*.

STEPHEN DUNN is the author of fourteen books of poetry, including the recently published *What Goes On: Selected and-- New Poems, 1995-2009*. His book *Different Hours* was awarded the Pulitzer Prize in 2001. He lives in Frostburg, Maryland.

TOM DVORSKE's work has appeared in *Sentence, Passages North, Texas Review, Spork, Poems & Plays*, and *The Louisville Review*. He is the author of the chapbook *What You Know* (Lazy Frog Press, 2002). Currently, he lives in Lake Charles, Louisiana, with his wife and daughter.

AMY GERSTLER's twelve books include *Dearest Creature; Ghost Girl; Medicine; Nerve Storm*; and *Bitter Angel*, which was awarded the National Book Critics Circle Award in 1990. Her nonfiction has appeared in *The Village Voice, Bookforum, Artforum, Los Angeles Magazine*, and numerous other publications. She is a core faculty member at the Bennington Writing Seminars, Bennington College, Vermont, and lives in Los Angeles, California.

JACK GILBERT is the author of *Refusing Heaven*, winner of the National Book Critics Circle Award in 2006; *The Great Fires: Poems 1982-1992; Monolithos*, which was short-listed for the Pulitzer Prize; and *Views of Jeoparder*, the 1962 winner of the Yale Younger Poets Prize. He lives in Northampton, Massachusetts.

LINDA GREGG is the author of seven poetry collections: *Too Bright to See; Alma; The Sacraments of Desire; Chosen by the Lion; Things and Flesh; In the Middle Distance*; and *All of It Singing: New and Selected Poems*. In 2006, she received the PEN/Voelcker Award in Poetry for career achievement. She lives in New York City.

BETH GYLYS is an Associate Professor at Georgia State University. She has published two collections of poetry—*Spot in the Dark* (Ohio State University Press, 2004) and *Bodies That Hum* (Silverfish Review Press, 1999). Her work has appeared in such journals as *The Paris Review, Antioch Review, Kenyon Review*, and *Ploughshares*.

MARK HALLIDAY teaches at Ohio University. His fifth book of poems, *Keep This Forever*, was published by Tupelo Press in 2008.

JAMES HARMS is the author of five collections of poetry: *After West, Freeways and Aqueducts, Quarters, The Joy Addict*, and *Modern Ocean* (all published by Carnegie Mellon University Press). His awards include a National Endowment for the Arts Fellowship, three Pushcart Prizes, and the PEN/Revson Fellowship. He founded and now directs the M.F.A. Program in Creative Writing at West Virginia University, where he is a Professor of English. He also directs New England College's M.F.A. Program in Poetry.

ROBERT HASS's books of poetry include *Time and Materials*, which won the 2007 National Book Award; *Sun Under Wood: New Poems; Human Wishes*, which won the National Book Critics Circle Award in 1996; *Praise*; and *Field Guide*, winner of the 1973 Yale Younger Poets Prize. He served as Poet Laureate of the United States from 1995 to 1997. He lives in California with his wife and teaches at the University of California, Berkeley.

BOB HICOK's most recent collection, *This Clumsy Living* (University of Pittsburgh Press, 2007), was awarded the 2008 Bobbitt Prize from the Library of Congress. His other books include *Insomnia Diary* (Pitt, 2004); *Animal Soul* (Invisible Cities Press, 2001), a finalist for the National Book Critics Circle Award; *Plus Shipping* (BOA, 1998); and *The Legend of Light* (University of Wisconsin, 1995), which received the Felix Pollak Prize in Poetry and was named a 1997 ALA Booklist Notable Book of the Year. A recipient of three Pushcart Prizes, a Guggenheim, and two National Endowment for the Arts Fellowships, his work has been selected for inclusion in five volumes of *Best American Poetry*.

EDWARD HIRSCH's most recent book of poems is *Special Orders*. He is President of the John Simon Guggenheim Memorial Foundation.

TONY HOAGLAND has published three collections of poetry: most recently, *What Narcissism Means to Me*, from Graywolf Press. He teaches at the University of Houston and in the low residency program at Warren Wilson College.

CYNTHIA HUNTINGTON's most recent book of poems, *The Radiant*, was published by Four Way Books in 2003. She has also published a prose memoir, *The Salt House*. She lives in Vermont and is a Professor of English at Dartmouth College. Her latest work in progress, set in the dunes of Provincetown, is titled *White Heat: A Hallucinatory Memoir*.

DENIS JOHNSON is the author of several novels, plays, and books of verse. His novel, *Tree of Smoke*, won the 2007 National Book Award.

ROBERT KELLY has published more than fifty collections of poetry, including *Kill the Messenger Who Brings Bad News*; *Red Actions: Selected Poems, 1960-1993*; *Lapis*; and *Under Words*. He has received an Award for Distinction from the National Academy and Institute of Arts and Letters and a National Endowment for the Arts Fellowship. He currently serves as Asher B. Edelman Professor of Literature and Co-Director of the Program in Written Arts at Bard College, where he has taught since 1961.

YUSEF KOMUNYAKAA's many books include *Pleasure Dome: New and Collected Poems, 1975-1999* and *Blue Notes: Essays, Interviews and Commentaries*. He has received a Pulitzer Prize, a National Endowment for the Arts Fellowship, and the Kingsley Tufts Poetry Award. He lives in New York City, where he is Distinguished Senior Poet in New York University's Graduate Creative Writing Program.

MAXINE KUMIN's sixteenth collection of poetry, *Still to Mow*, published by W.W. Norton & Company, Inc., in 2007, has just come out in paperback. Her awards include the Pulitzer Prize, the Ruth Lilly Poetry Prize, the Aiken Taylor Award, the Robert Frost Medal, and the Paterson Prize. From 1981 to 1982, she served as Poet Laureate of the United States. Currently, she and her husband live on a farm in Warner, New Hampshire.

DAVID LEHMAN's latest books are *A Fine Romance: Jewish Songwriters, American Songs* (Nextbook/Schocken) and *Yeshiva Boys*, a collection of poems (Scribner). He is the editor of *The Oxford Book of American Poetry*, the series editor of *The Best American Poetry*, and the author of such books as *Signs of the Times: Deconstruction and the Fall of Paul de Man* and *The Daily Mirror: A Journal in Poetry*. He lives in New York City.

DONNA MASINI is the author of two collections of poems—*Turning to Fiction* (W.W. Norton & Company, 2004) and *That Kind of Danger* (W.W. Norton & Company, 1998). Her poems have appeared in such journals as *American Poetry Review, Open City, TriQuarterly, The Paris Review*, and *Parnassus*. A recipient of a National Endowment for the Arts Fellowship, a New York Foundation for the Arts Grant, and a Pushcart Prize, she is an Associate Professor of English at Hunter College. She lives in New York City.

JANE MILLER's 2008 book, *Midnights*, is Saturnalia Press's artist/poet Collaboration Series #4 (with visual art contributed by Beverly Pepper and an introduction by C.D. Wright). Her other recent work is the book-length sequence, *A Palace of Pearls* (Copper Canyon Press, 2005), which received the 2006 Audre Lorde Prize in Poetry. Among her earlier collections are *Wherever You Lay Your Head; Memory at These Speeds: New & Selected Poems; The Greater Leisures*, a National Poetry Series Selection; and *August Zero*, winner of the Western States Book Award. She has also written *Working Time: Essays on Poetry, Culture, and Travel*, published in the University of Michigan's Poets on Poetry Series.

STEVE ORLEN has published six books of poetry. His most recent is *The Elephant's Child: New & Selected Poems, 1978-2005* (Ausable Press, 2006). He teaches in the low residency M.F.A. Program at Warren Wilson College and at the University of Arizona in Tucson.

KEVIN PRUFER's books include *Little Paper Sacrifice*, forthcoming from Four Way Books; *National Anthem* (Four Way, 2008); and *Fallen from a Chariot* (Carnegie Mellon University Press, 2005). He is the editor of *New European Poets* (Graywolf, 2008) and *Pleiades: A Journal of New Writing*. The recipient of three Pushcart Prizes, he teaches at the University of Central Missouri and lives out in the country.

MARTHA RHODES is the author of three collections of poetry: *At the Gate, Perfect Disappearance*, and *Mother Quiet*. She teaches at Sarah Lawrence College and in the M.F.A. Program at Warren Wilson College. She is also the founding editor and director of Four Way Books.

J. ALLYN ROSSER's third collection of poems, *Foiled Again*, won the 2007 New Criterion Poetry Prize and was published by Ivan R. Dee. Her previous books are *Misery Prefigured* and *Bright Moves*. She has received numerous awards for her work, among them the Morse Poetry Prize, the Peter I. B. Lavan Award for Younger Poets from the Academy of American Poets, the Wood and Frederick Bock Prize from *Poetry*, and Fellowships from the National Endowment for the Arts and the Ohio Arts Council. Rosser currently teaches at Ohio University.

MICHAEL RYAN has published four books of poems, an autobiography, a memoir, and a collection of essays about poetry and writing. He has been a National Book Award Finalist and the winner of the Lenore Marshall Prize and the Kingsley Tufts Award.

RAVI SHANKAR is Associate Professor and Poet-in-Residence at Central Connecticut State University and founding editor of the international online journal of the arts, *Drunken Boat* (www.drunkenboat.com). He has published one book of poems, *Instrumentality* (Cherry Grove Collections, 2004), and, more recently, co-edited *Language for a New Century: Contemporary Poetry from Asia, the Middle East and Beyond* (Norton, 2008).

ALAN SHAPIRO, a member of the American Academy of Arts and Sciences, has published ten books of poetry: most recently, *Old War* (Houghton Mifflin, 2008). He has won the Kingsley Tufts Award, two National Endowment for the Arts Fellowships, and a Guggenheim, among other prestigious awards. Since 1995, he has taught in the Department of English and Comparative Literature at the University of North Carolina.

RICHARD SHELTON is a Regents' Professor in the University of Arizona Creative Writing Program. He is also the author of eleven books of poetry and two memoirs. In 2000, he received a grant from the Lannan Foundation for the commitment he has made, over the last thirty-five years, to developing and directing writing workshops in the Arizona state prison system.

PATRICIA SMITH is the author of five books of poetry, including *Blood Dazzler*, a 2008 National Book Award finalist, and *Teahouse of the Almighty*, winner of the 2007 Paterson Poetry Prize. She is a Pushcart Prize winner, a Cave Canem faculty member, and a four-time individual champion of the National Poetry Slam. She teaches at the College of Staten Island and in the Stonecoast M.F.A. Program at the University of Southern Maine.

MARK STRAND is the author of numerous collections of poetry, including *Man and Camel*, *Blizzard of One*, *Dark Harbor*, and *Reasons for Moving*. His honors include the Pulitzer Prize, the Bollingen Prize, three National Endowment for the Arts Fellowships, a MacArthur Foundation Award, and the Edgar Allen Poe Prize from the Academy of American Poets. He teaches English and Comparative Literature at Columbia University and lives in New York City.

JAMES TATE's latest book is *Ghost Soldiers*. He has received the Pulitzer Prize, the National Book Award, the William Carlos Williams Award, and Fellowships from the Guggenheim Foundation and the National Endowment for the Arts. He teaches at the University of Massachusetts.